# MORTARS AND ROCKETS

# Mortars and Rockets

## PETER CHAMBERLAIN AND TERRY GANDER

MACDONALD AND JANE'S
LONDON

Copyright © 1975 Peter Chamberlain and Terry Gander

*This book, or parts thereof, must not be reproduced in any form without permission.*

*First published in Great Britain in 1975 by*
*Macdonald and Jane's (Macdonald & Co. (Publishers) Ltd.)*
*Paulton House, 8 Shepherdess Walk, London N1 7LW*

Printed by Tinling (1973) Limited, Prescot, Merseyside
(a member of the Oxley Printing Group Ltd.)

ISBN 0 356 08080 3

# Introduction

In 1939 the mortar and the rocket were regarded as modern additions to the armouries of nations but they could both trace their ancestry back to the discovery of gunpowder in the early Middle Ages. Early cannon ball-firing devices were often of the short, smooth-bored and high angle firing variety, and these early 'pots' eventually evolved into the mortar or bombard. The mortar was usually kept as a specialised shell-firing weapon and in time grew so specialised that it fell into general disuse after the Napoleonic wars. After a brief flurry of service in the Crimea, mortars fell from favour as a weapon until the trench warfare of the First World War bought them back into use. But the mortar that was in service in 1939 was a different weapon from the early trench devices. In the years after 1918 it had grown into a light, handy infantry support weapon that was simple, accurate and relatively cheap, It was also light and mobile and could thus be bought into action quickly, fire off a few accurate rounds, and be gone before any retaliation could be made. The mortar was thus a most useful and handy infantry weapon and most of the mortars of World War 2 were used by the infantry.

Most mortars used during 1939-1945 fell into three main categories. At the bottom end of the scale were the platoon or squad weapons. More often referred to as grenade launchers than mortars, they were usually about 50 mm in calibre and used triggers for firing. Most used a gas escape port to vary the relatively short range. The second and most numerous group were the company mortars, of which the classic example must be the French Brandt 81 mm family. Brandt mortars were sold to and copied by nearly all the combatant nations. Firing a seven pound bomb to a range of about 3000 yards, the 81 mm mortars were loaded from the muzzle of the smooth-bored barrel. The bomb was allowed to fall until it struck a fixed firing pin which ignited the charge round the tail of the bomb. The bomb was then fired upwards along the barrel into a high trajectory and it fell down onto its target. Range changes were made by altering the angle of elevation. The heavy mortars were usually kept at battalion level or even higher and were used for heavy fire support. Calibres started around 90-100 mm and the heaviest often had the extra luxuries of rifled barrels and breech-loading. Typical of this group was the Russian 120-HM 38, one of the best designs in use during the Second World War. It fired a 35 lb bomb to a range of 6500 yards.

Of the all combatant nations, the greatest exponents of the mortar were the Russians and the Germans. The Russians used the mortar in large numbers, mainly to conserve their resources for manufacturing heavier artillery weapons, but also because the mortar required less training and manufacturing 'back-up' than artillery. The German approach was similar but they tended to produce more refined weapons than the Russians and gradually fell behind in the technical race to provide mortars in increasingly heavier calibres. They made up for this deficiency only by copying Russians designs and using large numbers of captured weapons. The British and Americans tended to be more conservative in their approach to mortars but as the war went on both nations used increasing numbers and developed heavier calibres. The Japanese did the same but they tended to use the mortar as a substitute for heavy guns which they were unable to produce in sufficient numbers.

Like the mortar the rocket is a very old weapon that came back into prominence during the years between the wars. The first recorded use of the rocket was in 1232, but it was not introduced into the European armoury in any numbers until after about 1750. After the Napoleonic wars it fell into disuse and only came back into prominence during the early 1930s when research into new rocket propellants started in Russia, Germany and the UK. The new double-based propellants had the advantage over the old black powder used until then in that it could be cast in single pieces, or grains, and could be handled and stored with safety and reliability. By 1941 both Germany and Russia had large numbers of rocket equipments in service both as artillery and anti-aircraft weapons. The rockets used tended to fall into two main groups. Most numerous were the simple fin-stabilised rockets which were cheap to produce but had a greater dispersion and thus degree of inaccuracy then the second group which were the spin-stabilised rockets. These were stabilised by spinning the rocket using venturii in the rocket exhaust. Although they were much more accurate they were more expensive and difficult to produce. The Germans were the greatest exponent of the 'spinners' while the Russians used the 'finners,' as did the British who pressed the rocket into use as an anti-aircraft weapon to bolster their lack of guns. The Americans started the war with no rockets in service but their massive industrial background soon made up for lost time and began to produce rockets in millions in all calibres. They produced what was probably the most widely used of all rockets in action during World War 2, namely the 4.5 inch M8 rocket. The word 'probably' is used because very little is known about the Russian rockets. They were kept under a veil of secrecy throughout the war and after, and even today little is known of them. For this reason the section on Russian rockets is short and incomplete. Japanese rockets were another section of their efforts to provide a substitute for heavy artillery. For this reason they tended to use them in ones and twos as heavy mortars, rather than the massed formations saturating large areas which was the normal German and Russian method. But Japanese industry never could supply the demand and Japanese rockets were often crude and their launchers hasty improvisations.

The mortar and the rocket both have definite tactical advantages. The mortar can accurately lay down fire on concealed and dug-in positions with a minimum of cost and time. It is mobile and has a high rate of fire. However, it has a relatively short range and cannot deliver fire horizontally and can thus be regarded only as a supplement to artillery and not a replacement. The rocket has the advantage that it requires a minimum of training and skill to use and has a heavy offensive load. It is relatively cheap to use and manufacture but its cost against a conventional artillery round is high as it is inherently inaccurate. It thus has to be used in large numbers in order to hit a target but is often used to saturate large areas with explosive or smoke. Perhaps the rocket's gravest disadvantage is its relatively short range combined with the debris and smoke produced when fired, especially when used en masse. This invites retaliatory fire which often reduces the rocket to a one-shot weapon.

The Second World War was the testing ground for both the infantry mortar and the modern rocket. The success of both can be measured by the fact that in 1974 both weapons still enjoy prominence in the armouries of both the East and the West.

*Photo Credits*

Imperial War Museum
U.S. Official
Ian Hogg
Bundesarchiv
K. R. Pawlas

# Mortars

## BELGIUM

### Lance Grenades de 50 mm DBT

This small Belgian grenade discharger was issued to infantry units at platoon level to add firepower to the unit in the assault. For its type it was rather complex in that it used a cartridge method of firing via a trigger operated by a lanyard. Range was rather limited and the bomb rather small, but it had little chance to prove itself in action due to the Belgian surrender of 1940. The stocks that fell into German hands were issued to occupying Forces as the 5 cm Granatwerfer 201 (b), but very few were used.

**Data**

| | |
|---|---|
| CALIBRE 50 mm 1.97 in | ELEVATION 30° to 50° |
| BARREL LENGTH 200 mm 7.87 in | M.V. 75 m/s 246 ft/sec |
| BORE LENGTH 190 mm 7.48 in | MAXIMUM RANGE 585 m 640 yards |
| WEIGHT IN ACTION 7.7 kg 16.98 lb | BOMB WEIGHT 0.6 kg 1.32 lb |

*Lance Grenades de 50 mm DBT*

## CZECHOSLOVAKIA

### 8 cm minomet vz. 36

*8 cm minomet vz. 36*

This mortar was a Czech variant of the French 81 mm Brandt mortar and should not be confused with the Czech license-built version of the French weapon. The licence-built version was the 8.14 cm minomet which was used by the Germans as the 8.14 cm GrW 278 (t). The Czech derivative used a slightly smaller calibre and different ammunition. An automatic loading device holding six bombs in a rotary drum device fixed to the muzzle was developed for the vz.36 but saw little, if any, service. The Germans took over the vz.36 in 1938 and used it as the 8 cm GrW M.36 (t).

**Data**

| | |
|---|---|
| CALIBRE 81.3 mm 3.2 in | MINIMUM RANGE (heavy bomb) 40 m 44 yards |
| BARREL LENGTH (L/14) 1165 mm 45.86 in | MAXIMUM RANGE (light bomb) 3400 m 3720 yards |
| WEIGHT 62 kg 136.7 lb | |
| ELEVATION +40° to +80° | MAXIMUM RANGE (heavy bomb) 1200 m 1313 yards |
| TRAVERSE 10° | |
| M.V. (max) 220 m/s 722 ft/sec | BOMB WEIGHT (light) 3.26 kg 7.19 lb |
| MINIMUM RANGE (light bomb) 80 m 87 yards | BOMB WEIGHT (heavy) 6.85 kg 15.1 lb |

### 9 cm Lehký minomet vz. 17

This was an old Skoda design which was still in service when the Germans took over Czechoslovakia. Although there are no records of the Germans using this weapon it is likely that they remained emplaced as fortress weapons for some years.

**Data**

| | |
|---|---|
| CALIBRE 90 mm 3.54 in | TRAVERSE 120° |
| BARREL LENGTH (L/9) 810 mm 31.9 in | MINIMUM RANGE 300 m 328 yards |
| WEIGHT 132 kg 291 lb | MAXIMUM RANGE 1990 m 2177 yards |
| ELEVATION 45° to 70° | BOMB WEIGHT 6.2 kg 13.67 lb |

*9 cm lehky minomet vz. 17*

## 14 cm hrubý minomet vz. 18

This heavy Skoda mortar was taken over by the Germans in 1938 as the 14 cm Minenwerfer 18 (t). They appear to have used it mainly as a static defence or coastal weapon.

There was a 10.5 cm horsky minomet 'B11' but it was not developed beyond the prototype stage.

### Data

| | | | |
|---|---|---|---|
| CALIBRE | 140 mm | 5.5 in | |
| BARREL LENGTH (L/9) | 1260 mm | 49.6 in | |
| WEIGHT | 387.5 kg | 854.4 lb | |
| ELEVATION | 45° to 75° | | |
| TRAVERSE | 135° | | |
| MINIMUM RANGE | 475 m | 520 yards | |
| MAXIMUM RANGE | 2680 m | 2932 yards | |
| BOMB WEIGHT | 15 kg | 33.1 lb | |

# FRANCE

## Lance Grenades de 50 mm Modèle 37

The Mle 37 was issued in 1939 to replace the French rifle grenades then in use at platoon level. It used a fixed 45° elevation with range variation bought about by altering the diameter of gas vents. Small and very light it was a useful weapon but the maximum range was only 460 m and the bomb was light. Not many appear to have been used in action, but the Germans used some as the 5 cm Granatwerfer 203 (f).

### Data

| | | | |
|---|---|---|---|
| CALIBRE | 50 mm | 1.97 in | |
| BARREL LENGTH | 415 mm | 16.34 in | |
| BORE LENGTH | 280 mm | 11 in | |
| WEIGHT | 3.65 kg | 8.05 lb | |
| ELEVATION | 45°—fixed | | |
| TRAVERSE | 8° | | |
| M.V. (max) | 70 m/s | 230 ft/sec | |
| MINIMUM RANGE | 70 m | 76.6 yards | |
| MAXIMUM RANGE | 460 m | 503 yards | |
| BOMB WEIGHT | 0.435 kg | 0.96 lb | |

*Lance Grenades de 50 mm Modele 37*

## Mortier de 60 mm Modèle 1935

The 60 mm Mle 35 was one of the many products of the Edgar Brandt design bureau and it entered French service in 1937. It was entirely conventional in design and construction and became the American Mortar 60 mm M1 (and from that the M2 and M19). The Chinese copied it as the Type 31 with a slightly shorter barrel Large numbers of the Mle 35 fell into German hands in 1940 and they were used by them for second-line units in France as the 6 cm Granatwerfer 225 (f). In 1940 the French had 4940 Mle 35 mortars in service.

### Data

| | | | |
|---|---|---|---|
| CALIBRE | 60.7 mm | 2.39 in | |
| BARREL LENGTH | 724 mm | 28.5 in | |
| BORE LENGTH | 655 mm | 25.8 in | |
| WEIGHT IN ACTION | 17.8 kg | 39.25 lb | |
| ELEVATION | 45° to 85° | | |
| TRAVERSE | 5° to 12°—variable with elevation | | |
| M.V. (max) | 158 m/s | 518 ft/sec | |
| MAXIMUM RANGE (light bomb) | 1700 m | 1860 yards | |
| MAXIMUM RANGE (heavy bomb) | 950 m | 1040 yards | |
| BOMB WEIGHT (light) | 1.3 kg | 2.87 lb | |
| BOMB WEIGHT (heavy) | 2.2 kg | 4.85 lb | |

*Mortier de 60 mm Modèle 1935*

*Mortier de 60 mm Modèle 1935 on manoeuvres in Southern England with the Free French in August 1940*

# Mortier Brandt de 81 mm Modele 27/31

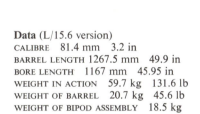

*Mortier Brandt de 81 mm Modèle 27/31*

The 81 mm mortar produced by the French Brandt firm became the 'classic'design of its era for it was copied or licence-built by almost every army in Europe and else-where. It remains to this day the epitome of conventional mortar design and for this reason the data is given in more detail. In 1940 the French had over 8000 in service in two main versions—one with a L/15.6 barrel and a shorter L/13.7 version. Listed below are the main users other than France with German designations where appropriate:

**Austria:** *8 cm GrW 33 (ö)*
**China:**
**Czechosolovakia:** 81.4 mm minomet *8 cm GrW 278 (t)*
**Denmark:** 81.4 mm L/12  *8.14 cm GrW 275 (d)*
**Finland:** 81 mm Tampella
**Germany:** 8.14 cm Granatwerfer 278 (f) und 278/1 (f)
**Italy:** 81/14 modello 35  *8.1 cm GrW 276(i)*

**Japan:** 81 mm Type 3
**Jugoslavia:** 8.1 cm M W M 31/38 Kragujewac  *8.14 cm GrW 270 (j)*
**Netherlands:** Mortier van 8 *8.14 cm GrW 286(h)*
**Poland:** wz.31  *8 cm GrW 31(p)*
**USA:** 81 mm Mortar M1
**USSR:** 82 mm Model 1936 *8.2 cm GrW 274/1(r)*

**Data** (L/15.6 version)
CALIBRE  81.4 mm  3.2 in
BARREL LENGTH 1267.5 mm  49.9 in
BORE LENGTH  1167 mm  45.95 in
WEIGHT IN ACTION  59.7 kg  131.6 lb
WEIGHT OF BARREL  20.7 kg  45.6 lb
WEIGHT OF BIPOD ASSEMBLY  18.5 kg 40.8 lb
WEIGHT OF BASE PLATE  20.5 kg  45.2 lb
ELEVATION  45° to 85°
TRAVERSE  8° to 12°—variable with elevation
M.V.  174 m/s  571 ft/sec
MAXIMUM RANGE (light bomb)  2850 m 3118 yards
MAXIMUM RANGE (heavy bomb)  1200 m 1313 yards
BOMB WEIGHT (light)  3.25 kg  7.17 lb
BOMB WEIGHT (heavy)  6.5 kg  14.3 lb

The German weapons were captured from the French in 1940. Many Brandt mortars from most of the sources listed above were used by the Germans either as front-line weapons or coastal defence weapons.

*Danish 81.4 mm L/12*

*Modèle 27/31 in action*

*Dutch Mortier van 8*

*Polish wz.31 in action*

# GERMANY

## 5 cm leichte Granatwerfer 36

The standard light mortar of the German forces during the early war years was the 5 cm le.Gr.W.36, a small, handy and rather complex weapon. It was carried into action by two men and levelling and elevation controls were directly fitted onto the baseplate. Elevation controls provided were coarse and fine and up to 1938 a rather complex and awkward telescopic sight was used. This was later dispensed with in favour of a simple white line on the barrel for alignment. A trigger was used for firing and only HE ammunition was used. For all its complexity the performance of the le.Gr.W.36 was not outstanding and it was gradually replaced by the kz.8 cm Gr.W.42. After 1942 the le.Gr.W.36 was withdrawn from front-line service and was used only by second-line and reserve units.

**Data**
CALIBRE   5 cm   1.969 in
BARREL LENGTH   465 mm   18.3 in
BORE LENGTH   350 mm   13.78 in
WEIGHT IN ACTION   14 kg   30.8 lb
ELEVATION   42° to 20°
TRAVERSE   34°
M.V.   75 m/s   246 ft/sec
MINIMUM RANGE   60 m   65 yards
MAXIMUM RANGE   520 m   569 yards
BOMB WEIGHT   0.9 kg   1.98 lb
50% ZONE AT MAXIMUM   31 × 4 m
   33.9 × 4.4 yards

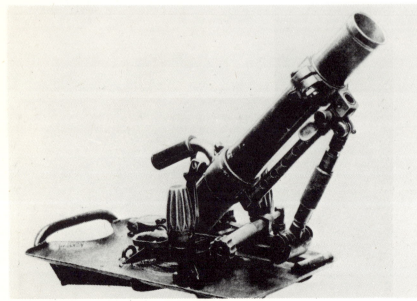

*5 cm leichte Granatwerfer 36*

*5 cm leGrW in action*

# 8 cm schwerer Granatwerfer 34

**Data**
CALIBRE  81.4 mm  3.2 in
BARREL LENGTH  1143 mm  45 in
BORE LENGTH  1033 mm  40.67 in
WEIGHT IN ACTION  56.7 kg  125 lb
ELEVATION  40° to 90°
TRAVERSE  9° to 15°—variable with
  elevation
M.V. (Charge 1)  75 m/s  246 ft/sec
M.V. (Charge 5)  174 m/s  571 ft/sec
MINIMUM RANGE  60 m  65.6 yards
MAXIMUM RANGE  2400 m  2625 yards
EFFECTIVE RANGE  400 to 1200 m
  437 to 1312 yards
50% ZONE AT MAXIMUM  65 × 14 m
  71 × 15 yards
BOMB WEIGHT  3.5 kg  7.72 lb

**Self propelled Carriages**
SdKfz 250/7 Gr. W. Wagen
  (Granatwerferwagen)
SdKfz 251/2 mittler Schützenpanzerwagen
  (Granatwerfer)
8 cm schwerer Granatwerfer 34 auf
PzSpWg AMR(f)

*8 cm sGrW 34 in action in Russia*

The s.Gr.W.34 entered service in 1934 and remained in service until 1945. In all respects it was a conventional and unremarkable mortar but as it remained the standard heavy infantry mortar of the front-line troops throughout the war it gained for itself a reputation for accuracy and firepower which should have gone to the well-trained and efficient crews that manned it. It was carried into action as a three-man load—base plate, barrel and bipod—but it could also be carried on a pack mule, sledge or vehicle. A wide range of bombs was developed for this mortar including the 8 cm Wurfgranate 39 'bouncing bomb'. Other rounds were conventional HE, smoke, target illumination and target marking, fired by a combination of one primary and four secondary charges. The general standard of manufacture of the s.Gr.W.34 was first class and it was a very sturdy and popular weapon. A RA 35 dial sight was used. To increase the weapons tactical mobility the s.Gr.W.34 was fitted to special half-track vehicles. It was gradually supplemented in infantry units by the 12 cm Gr.W.42.

*SdKfz 250/7 (Granatwerferwagen)*

*1, 2.* 8 cm schwerer Granatwerfer 34

1

2

# Kurzer 8 cm Granatwerfer 42 (Stummelwerfer)

The kz.8 cm Gr.W.42 was originally intended for use by airborne and special purpose units but it gradually replaced the small 5 cm le.Gr.W.34 as the standard light infantry mortar. It was a shortened and lightened version of the 8 cm s.Gr.W.34 that fired standard 8 cm ammunition, and it was bought into action as a three-man load. The short barrel meant a decrease in range but the heavier bomb meant an increase in infantry firepower as opposed to the 5 cm weapon. One extra that was sometimes fitted to this mortar was a lanyard operated loading mechanism which fitted over the reinforced muzzle. A bomb could be inserted into this mechanism and held there until released and fired by the lanyard—this enabled the crew to take cover in an ambush situation and fire the mortar remotely. The ammunition was fired by a combination of one primary and two secondary charges.

**Data**

| | | |
|---|---|---|
| CALIBRE | 81.4 mm | 3.2 in |
| BARREL LENGTH | 747 mm | 29.4 in |
| BORE LENGTH | 650 mm | 25.6 in |
| WEIGHT IN ACTION | 26.5 kg | 58.4 lb |
| ELEVATION | 40° to 90° | |
| TRAVERSE | 14° to 34°—variable with elevation | |
| MINIMUM RANGE | 50 m | 55 yards |
| MAXIMUM RANGE | 1100 m | 1203 yards |
| BOMB WEIGHT | 3.5 kg | 7.72 lb |

*Kurzer 8 cm Granatwerfer 42*

# 10 cm Nebelwerfer 35

The 10 cm Nebelwerfer 35 was the standard smoke and chemical mortar used by the German Nebeltruppen, whose task was to provide smoke and gas coverage on the battlefield. After 1941 the Nb 35 was phased out of service with the Nebeltruppen and replaced by the 15 and 21 cm Nebelwerfer rocket equipments, but it continued in service as a conventional HE mortar. It was a scaled-up version of the 8 cm s.Gr.W.34 and used a five-man crew. The only difference (apart from size) from the 8 cm weapon was in the traversing gear where the screw was contained in a sleeve. By changing the firing pin the Nb35 could fire the heavier Nb 40 ammunition, but normal Nb 35 rounds were smoke, HE and incendiary. Gas bombs were available but were not used. When on the move the Nb 35 was carried in a small hand-cart, but sledges and pack animals were also used.

**Data**

| | | |
|---|---|---|
| CALIBRE | 105 mm | 4.14 in |
| BORE LENGTH | 1207 mm | 47.5 in |
| BARREL LENGTH | 1344 mm | 52.9 in |
| WEIGHT IN ACTION | 102.6 kg | 226.2 lb |
| ELEVATION | 45° to 90° | |
| TRAVERSE | 28° | |
| M.V. (Charge 1) | 105 m/s | 344 ft/sec |
| M.V. (Charge 3) | 193 m/s | 633 ft/sec |
| MINIMUM RANGE | 300 m | 328 yards |
| MAXIMUM RANGE | 3000 m | 3280 yards |
| 50% ZONE AT MAXIMUM | 53 × 21 m | 58 × 23 yards |
| BOMB WEIGHT | 7.36 kg | 16.2 lb |

*10 cm Nebelwerfer 35*

*10 cm NbW 35 in action*

# 10 cm Nebelwerfer 40

**Data**

CALIBRE  105 mm  4.14 in
BORE LENGTH (L/16)  1720 mm  67.7 in
WEIGHT IN ACTION (approx)  800 kg
   1764 lb
ELEVATION  45° to 84°
TRAVERSE  14°
M.V.  310 m/s  1017 ft/sec
MINIMUM RANGE  500 m  547 yards
MAXIMUM RANGE  6225-6350 m
   6810-6947 yards
50% ZONE AT MAXIMUM  137 × 49 m
   150 % 54 yards
BOMB WEIGHT (HE)  8.6 kg  18.96 lb
BOMB WEIGHT (smoke)  8.9 kg  19.6 lb

Relatively few examples of the 10 cm Nb 40 ever saw service with the Nebeltruppen for it entered service in 1940 just as the units for which it was intended were changing over to rocket equipments. It was a massive complex affair that featured a complicated breech loading mechanism not unlike that used on the 7.5 cm leIG 18. The main asset of the Nb 40 was its range of up to 6350 m which was of considerable value when the piece was called on to fire HE, but its primary purpose was firing smoke and chemical rounds. These rounds were propelled by using a short cartridge case loaded with a primary charge and up to three auxiliary charges. The main drawback of the Nb 40 was its cost—14,000 RM as opposed to 1,500 RM for the Nb 35. When on the move, the Nb 40 was towed on a two-wheeled carriage.

*10 cm Nebelwerfer 40*

*10 cm NbW 40 in action*

# 12 cm Granatwerfer 42

**Data**

CALIBRE  120 mm  4.72 in
BARREL LENGTH (L/15.5)  1865 mm
   73.4 in
BORE LENGTH  1540 mm  60.6 in
WEIGHT IN ACTION  285 kg  628.4 lb
ELEVATION  45° to 84°
TRAVERSE  8° to 17°—variable with
   elevation
M.V. (Charge 1)  122 m/s  400 ft/sec
M.V. (Charge 6)  283 m/s  928 ft/sec
MINIMUM RANGE  300 m  328 yards
MAXIMUM RANGE  6025 m  6591 yards
50% ZONE AT MAXIMUM  165 × 37 m
   180 × 40 yards
BOMB WEIGHT  15.8 kg  38.84 lb

The 12 cm Granatwerfer 42 was an almost direct copy of the Russian Model 38 heavy mortar which had been impressed into German service as the 12 cm Gr.W.378 (r). This weapon made a profound impression on the German front-line troops as it outranged and outclassed all the standard German mortars then in use, so it was not long before the Germans altered the Russian design to suit their own production methods and the 12 cm Gr.W.42 entered service in 1942. The Gr.W.42 featured a two-wheeled carriage which hinged on the base plate when in use and the firing mechanism could be either gravity percussion or a trigger arrangement. In action the base plate had to be dug in for prolonged use. Both Russian and German ammunition could be used and was fired by a primary charge and up to six secondary charges. The 12 cm.Gr.W.42 soon became a very popular and effective weapon in German hands and replaced many of the lighter mortars in use and even replaced infantry guns in some infantry support units.

*12 cm GrW 42 ready for action but still on its carriage*

*12 cm Granatwerfer 42 dismounted*

*12 cm GrW 42 in use against the Russians*

# 20 cm leichte Ladungswerfer

The 20 cm leichte Ladungswerfer was a specialised spigot mortar used by German engineers to clear obstacles and minefields. It consisted of a spigot over which a 20 cm diameter bomb was placed. A large base plate absorbed the recoil forces as in a conventional mortar, but a curved arm connected the spigot to the bipod assembly. Firing was carried out electrically from a distance, and up to three charges in a small cartridge propelled the rounds to a rather short range of about 700 m. The rounds were either a thin-walled HE bomb for demolishing strongpoints, a smoke bomb, or a specialised harpoon projectile—the Harpunengeschosse—which carried a rope across minefields. After the harpoon had landed the rope could be used to tow charges across the minefield to clear a path. The leichte Ladungswerfer was used in the 1940 campaigns and in North Africa but after that was hardly ever encountered.

There was an even heavier version of this weapon in the shape of the 38 cm schwere Ladungswerfer, but no records exist of its being used during World War 2.

**Data**

| | | |
|---|---|---|
| DIAMETER OF SPIGOT | 90 mm | 3.5 in |
| LENGTH OF SPIGOT | 540 mm | 21.26 in |
| WEIGHT IN ACTION | 93 kg | 205 lb |
| MAXIMUM RANGE (HE) | 700 m | 766 yards |
| BOMB WEIGHT (HE) | 21.27 kg | 46.9 lb |

*20 cm leichte Ladungswerfer unloaded*

*20 cm leLdW loaded with a bomb ready to fire*

# Mittler Schutzenpanzerwagen S307(f) mit Reihenwerfer

One specialised German adaptation of a vehicle to carry a unique mortar battery which deserves mention was the conversion of a French Somua half-track to carry a sixteen-barrel mortar battery. This battery was the Reihenwerfer, and it used 8.14 cm GrW 278 (f) barrels. The barrels were mounted in two rows of eight on the back of the half-track and were so arranged that all sixteen barrels could be elevated together. Traverse was 360° but the outer three barrels could be turned outwards a further few degrees to give a greater target coverage. In action the rounds were held by a mechanism just inside the barrel muzzles, and all were fired by pulling a lanyard to release the bombs. They were not fired simultaneously but in rapid succession. As far as can be discovered these batteries were used only in France and some saw action in 1944.

**Data**

WEIGHT OF VEHICLE COMPLETE    7118.7 kg
    15680 lb
LENGTH OF VEHICLE    5766 mm    227 in
WIDTH OF VEHICLE    2083 mm    82 in
HEIGHT OF BASIC VEHICLE    2032 mm    80 in
ELEVATION    35° to 90°
TRAVERSE    360°
AMMUNITION CARRIED    90 rounds

*Reihenwerfer*

# ITALY

## 45/5 modello 35 'Brixia'

To the Italians must go the prize for producing the most needlessly complicated light mortar in use by any of the World War 2 combatants. The little 45 mm Brixia mortar embodied a number of novel features including a magazine holding ten propelling cartridges and a gas port for varying range. The rounds were hand-fed into an open breech one at a time—closing the breech by hand automatically loaded a cartridge. The mounting was complex and incorporated elevation and traverse controls while a gunner's seat doubled as a back rest when the mortar and mount were folded for carrying. The weapon had a high fire rate and was very accurate but the light bomb was relatively ineffective due to poor fragmentation effects. Some were used by German troops in North Africa and Italy—they were designated 4.5 cm Granatwerfer 176 (i).

### Data

| | | | | |
|---|---|---|---|---|
| CALIBRE | 45 mm | 1.77 in | TRAVERSE | 20° |
| BARREL LENGTH (L/5.4) | 260 mm | 10.2 in | M.V. (max) | 83 m/s   272 ft/sec |
| BORE LENGTH | 241 mm | 9.49 in | MINIMUM RANGE | 322 m   352 yards |
| WEIGHT IN ACTION | 15.5 kg | 34.18 lb | MAXIMUM RANGE | 536 m   586 yards |
| ELEVATION | 10° to 90° | | BOMB WEIGHT | 0.465 kg   1.025 lb |

The modello 35 being carried in such a way that the seat forms a back pad

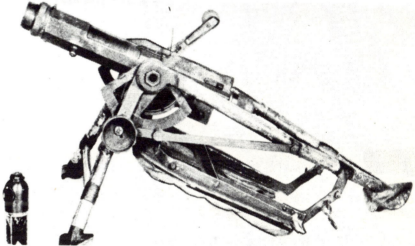

45/5 modello 35 'Brixia' with its diminutive bomb

Modello 35 in action in North Africa

# 81/14 modello 35

The Italians were also among the number of armies that copied the French 81mm mortar and added it to their armoury. The Italian version was the modello 35 and differed little from the original. It became the standard Italian infantry support mortar and was widely issued. Their allies the Germans also took over the modello 35 for their troops stationed in Italy and after 1943 took over even larger numbers. To the Germans it became the 8.1 cm Granatwerfer 276 (i), and it had the advantage that it could use standard German ammunition. In North Africa the modello 35 was often used by British units who valued its increased range when compared wiith their own 3-inch mortar.

**Data**

CALIBRE 81 mm 3.19 in
BARREL LENGTH (L/14.2) 1150 mm 45.28 in
WEIGHT IN ACTION 59 kg 130.1 lb
ELEVATION 40° to 90°
TRAVERSE 8°
M.V. (light bomb) 255 m/s 233 ft/sec
M.V. (heavy bomb) 135 m/s 124 ft/sec
MINIMUM RANGE (light bomb) 91 m 100 yards
MINIMUM RANGE (heavy bomb) 62 m 68 yards
MAXIMUM RANGE (light bomb) 4052 m 4429 yards
MAXIMUM RANGE (heavy bomb) 1500 m 1640 yards
BOMB WEIGHT (light) 3.265 kg 7.2 lb
BOMB WEIGHT (heavy) 6.865 kg 15.14 lb

*81/14 on manoeuvres—note the carrying frames used by the crew*

*81/14 captured in North Africa*

# JAPAN

## 50 mm Grenade Discharger Type 10

First produced in 1921 the Type 10 grenade discharger was the first of two grenade launchers used by the infantry to propel small grenades to a range of up to 175 yards. In use the spade base was placed on the ground and the barrel hand-held at an angle of 45°. Range was altered by opening a gas port—the wider the port the more the gas could escape and thus the range was reduced. Firing was accomplished by pulling on a lanyard which set off the trigger mechanism to detonate the propelling charge in the base of the grenade. The usual HE grenade was the Type 91, but there were smoke, flare and signal grenades. By 1941 the Type 10 had been largely replaced by the later Type 89, but the Type 10 was kept on for firing pyrotechnics. The Japanese designation was Junen Shiki Tekidanto, but to the Allies it was often referred to as the 'Knee mortar', an incorrect description that led to many broken legs.

**Data**

CALIBRE 50 mm 1.97 in
BARREL LENGTH 241 mm 9.5 in
OVERALL LENGTH 508 mm 20 in
WEIGHT 2.38 kg 5.25 lb
MINIMUM RANGE 60 m 65 yards
MAXIMUM RANGE 160 m 175 yards
BOMB WEIGHT 0.53 kg 1.17 lb

*50mm Grenade Discharger Type 10*

*Type 10 in action*

# 50 mm Grenade Discharger Type 89

The Type 89 grenade discharger first appeared in 1929 and differed from the earlier Type 10 in having a rifled barrel. Another difference was that the gas port was eliminated in favour of a firing pin that could be moved up and down the barrel to alter the range, and a larger curved base plate was fitted. The Type 91 grenade could be fired from this discharger but the more usual grenade was the Type 89 shell. Other possible rounds were smoke, incendiary, flare and signal grenades. The Type 89 could be fired to a range of 710 yards and was thus quite an addition to an infantry squad's firepower. Full Japanese designation was Hachikyu Shiki Jutekidanto. For use by paratroops a special version was developed that used a detachable baseplate.

**Data**

CALIBRE   50 mm   1.97 in
BARREL LENGTH   254 mm   10 in
OVERALL LENGTH   610 mm.   24 in
WEIGHT   4.65 kg   10.25 lb
MAXIMUM RANGE (Type 91)   190 m   208 yards
MINIMUM RANGE (Type 89)   120 m   131 yards
MAXIMUM RANGE (Type 89)   650 m   711 yards
BOMB WEIGHT (Type 89)   0.79 kg   1.75 lb

*Type 89 in action*

*50mm Grenade Discharger Type 89 with a Type 10 on the left for comparison*

# 50 mm Mortar Type 98

The 50 mm Mortar Type 98 entered service in 1938 and was a specialised demolition mortar. It consisted of a steel barrel preset to a fixed angle of 40° on a base plate, and it fired a stick grenade to a range of 455 yards. The stick grenade had a large square head that contained about 7 lb of picric acid blocks which could produce a considerable blast effect and were very useful in attacking and neutralising strong points during an attack. In use, the barrel was loaded with a black powder charge in a silk bag. The 50 mm diameter stick was then loaded into the barrel to a preset depth—the more the depth, the greater the range. The charge was fired by pulling on a lanyard from a safe distance. As well as firing the stick grenade, the Type 98 could also fire a bangalore torpedo to clear minefields.

**Data**

CALIBRE   50 mm   1.97 in
BARREL LENGTH   650 mm   25.6 in
WEIGHT   22.5 kg   49.6 lb
ELEVATION   40°—fixed
TRAVERSE   7°
MAXIMUM RANGE (HE)   416 m   455 yards
BOMB WEIGHT   6.4 kg   14.1 lb

*50mm Mortar Type 98*

*Type 98 with scaled muzzle clamp for regulating range*

# 70 mm Mortar Type 11

The Japanese referred to their Type 11 mortar as a high angle infantry gun as it had a rifled barrel. However, it still used muzzle-loading and thus qualifies as a mortar. It was a rather heavy weapon best suited for use in static situations, and it fired grenades that were enlarged versions of those used in the Type 89 grenade discharger. Firing was by a percussion hammer. This mortar, the full Japanese designation for which was Juichinen Shiki Kyokusha Hoheiho, entered service in 1922 but by 1942 it had been withdrawn from general use.

**Data**
CALIBRE   70 mm   2.76 in
WEIGHT EMPLACED   60.7 kg   133.75 lb
ELEVATION   37° to 77°
TRAVERSE   23°
MAXIMUM RANGE (approx)   1555 m
   1700 yards
BOMB WEIGHT   2.1 kg   4.67 lb

*Type 11 in action in China*

*70 mm Mortar Type 11*

# 81 mm Mortar Type 3

The Type 3 81 mm mortar was a direct copy of the ubiquitous Stokes-Brandt design and was first issued in 1928. It closely resembled all the other 81 mm Brandt designs and there was little of note about this weapon, except that production was still continuing at Yokosuka Navy Arsenal in 1943.

**Data**

| | | | |
|---|---|---|---|
| CALIBRE   81.4 mm   3.2 in | | MAXIMUM ELEVATION   +85° | |
| BARREL LENGTH   1257 mm   49.5 in | | BOMB WEIGHT (HE)   3.27 kg   7.2 lb | |
| WEIGHT   74.8 kg   167 lb | | BOMB WEIGHT (HE)   6.5 kg   14.3 lb | |

# 81 mm Mortar Type 97

The Type 97, or to give the Japanese designation, the Shiki Kyokusha Hoheiho, was first issued in 1937 and was the revised 'Japanese' version of the Type 3 which was a copy of a French design. It was very similar to the Type 3 but was generally lighter, even though the same base plate as that fitted to the Type 3 was used. The main change was that the bore tolerances were very closely machined which led to a resultant retention of gases on firing. Thus, a shorter barrel could produce a better range than one with the usual amount of windage. The Type 97 became one of the two 'standard' Japanese infantry mortars and was encountered on all fronts.

**Data**

| | |
|---|---|
| CALIBRE   81 mm   3.19 in | MAXIMUM RANGE (7.2 lb)   3001 m   3280 yards |
| BARREL LENGTH   1257 mm   49.5 in | MAXIMUM RANGE (14.3 lb)   1200 m   1312 yards |
| BORE LENGTH   1162 mm   45.75 in | |
| WEIGHT   65.9 kg   145.125 lb | BOMB WEIGHT (HE)   3.27 kg   7.2 lb |
| MAXIMUM ELEVATION   +85° | BOMB WEIGHT (HE)   6.5 kg   14.3 lb |

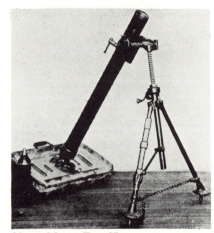
*81 mm Mortar Type 97*

# 81 mm Mortar Type 99

First issued in 1939, the Type 99 carried the close machining of the barrel first used on the Type 97 one stage further to produce a shorter and lighter weapon which had a performance identical to that of the longer Type 97. It also featured an alternative trigger mechanism which could be used instead of the normal fixed firing pin system. The Type 99, or Kyukyu Shiki Shohakugekiho, became the second of the 'standard' infantry mortars and was widely used. It fired the same ammunition as the Type 97.

**Data**

CALIBRE  81mm  3.19 in
BARREL LENGTH  641 mm  25.25 in
WEIGHT  23.7 kg  52.25 lb
MAXIMUM ELEVATION  +70°
MAXIMUM RANGE (7.2 lb)  3001 m
  3280 yards
MAXIMUM RANGE (14.3 lb)  1200 m
  1312 yards
BOMB WEIGHT (HE)  3.27 kg  7.2 lb
BOMB WEIGHT (HE)  6.5 kg  14.3 lb

*81 mm Mortar Type 99*

# 90 mm Mortar Type 94

Known to the Japanese as the Kyuyon Shiki Keihakugehiko, the Type 94 90 mm mortar entered service in 1934. It featured a heavy recoil mechanism and a heavily reinforced breech, and this added to the weight of the piece to such an extent that mobility was impaired. The Type 94 thus became more of a static defence weapon or was often used as an emplaced barrage mortar, for which purpose it was furnished with a more complex dial sight than was usually encountered on mortars. The Type 94 was gradually replaced by the lighter Type 97 90 mm mortar.

**Data**

CALIBRE  90 mm  3.54 in
BARREL LENGTH  1270 mm  50 in
BORE LENGTH  1219 mm  48 in
WEIGHT  155 kg  341.5 lb
MAXIMUM ELEVATION +70°
TRAVERSE  10°
MINIMUM RANGE  558 m  610 yards
MAXIMUM RANGE  3797 m  4150 yards
BOMB WEIGHT  5.22 kg  11.5 lb

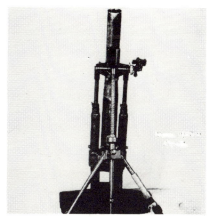

*90 mm Mortar Type 94 showing recoil cylinders on U-shaped frame*

*Type 94 in action*

# 90 mm Mortar Type 97

The 90 mm Type 97 was developed to replace the heavy Type 94, and it entered service in 1937. It dispensed with the recoil mechanism of the Type 94 but the bore length remained the same so the same range could be achieved as on the heavier weapon. The same base plate and bipod as that on the Type 94 were retained and the same ammunition was fired.

**Data**

| | | | | |
|---|---|---|---|---|
| CALIBRE | 90 mm | 3.54 in | MAXIMUM ELEVATION | +70° |
| BARREL LENGTH | 1330 mm | 52.375 in | TRAVERSE | 10° |
| BORE LENGTH | 1219 mm | 48 in | MINIMUM RANGE | 558 m 610 yards |
| WEIGHT | 105.8 kg | 233 lb | MAXIMUM RANGE | 3797 m 4150 yards |
| | | | BOMB WEIGHT | 5.22 kg 11.5 lb |

*90 mm Mortar Type 97*

*Type 97 in action in China*

# 150 mm Mortar Type 97

The largest and heaviest of the conventional Japanese mortars was the 150 mm Type 97. First issued in 1937 it was intended as a heavy bombardment weapon but as the war continued it was used as a coastal defence weapon, and some were mounted on 360° carriages on coastal craft. The general design was conventional and unremarkable except for its size.

**Data**

| | | | | |
|---|---|---|---|---|
| CALIBRE | 150 mm | 5.9 in | WEIGHT COMPLETE | 349.6 kg 770 lb |
| BARREL LENGTH | 1914.4 mm | 75.37 in | MAXIMUM ELEVATION | +80° |
| BORE LENGTH | 1676 mm | 66 in | MAXIMUM RANGE | 2001 m 2187 yards |
| | | | BOMB WEIGHT (HE) | 25.88 kg 57 lb |

*150 mm Mortar Type 97*

# POLAND

## 46 mm granatnik wz.36

**Data**

CALIBRE 46 mm 1.81 in
LENGTH OF BARREL 396 mm 15.6 in
LENGTH OVERALL 648 mm 25.5 in
WEIGHT COMPLETE 12.6 kg 27.8 lb
MINIMUM RANGE 100 m 109 yards
MAXIMUM RANGE 800 m 875 yards
BOMB WEIGHT 0.76 kg 1.67 lb
RATE OF FIRE (practical) 15 rpm

The design work on this indigenous Polish grenade launcher began in 1932 and went on until 1933. They were tried out on manoeuvres with the Polish Army and production began in 1936. The first issues were made to the Army in 1937 and in 1939 there were 3850 in service. The official establishment was three per company which meant 81 to a division. One man could carry the weapon on a shoulder sling. In design, the granatnik followed fairly conventional lines but the gas vent that varied the range was routed through an escape tube mounted over the barrel. After 1939 the little granatnik appears to have vanished from the scene.

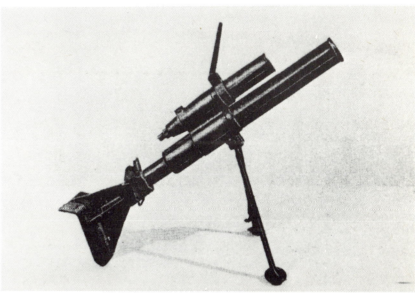

*46 mm granatnik wz. 36*

# UNITED KINGDOM

## Ordnance, M.L. 2-inch Mortar

*2-inch Mortar in its original Mark II form*

*Ordnance, M.L. 2-inch Mortar Mark 11\*\*\**

The first 2-inch mortar appeared in the trenches in 1918 but was declared obsolete in 1919. During the mid-1930s the need for a light mortar at infantry squad level was appreciated and a contest was held to determine the best design. The winner was a Spanish Ecia design which was modified and put into production in Feburary 1938. After that a wide and bewildering number of Marks and sub-Marks were produced. In an attempt to simplify the number of types produced by 1945 a list of the main variants follows:

| | |
|---|---|
| Mark 1 | — 1918 version, obsolete in 1919. |
| Mark 11 | — Initial 1938 version with base plate. |
| Mark 11* | — Universal carrier. |
| Mark 11** | — Universal carrier. |
| Mark 11*** | — Infantry. |
| Mark 111 | — Tank version. |
| Mark 1V | — Pilot production only. |
| Mark V | — Not manufactured. |
| Mark V1 | — Not manufactured. |
| Mark V11 | — Universal carrier. |
| Mark V11* | — Airborne. |
| Mark V11** | — Infantry. |

Mark V11A — Indian Army version.
Mark V111 — Airborne.
Mark V111* — Infantry.

As a rough guide, the Infantry versions used a small base spade as opposed to the versions for use on the Universal Carrier which had a heavier rectangular base plate. The Airborne versions were shorter and lighter. They all used the same ammunition which was produced in HE, smoke, illuminating and a wide variety of signal flares. In action the 2-inch mortar was hand-held at the required angle of elevation with the base spade or plate on the ground. The bombs were muzzle-loaded and trigger-fired. The trigger-firing had the advantage that bombs could be fired horizontally which was very useful in houseclearing and close fighting. They were usually issued one to a platoon but this was often exceeded. In 1974 the 2-inch mortar is still in service.

**Data (II*** & VII*)**

| | | | |
|---|---|---|---|
| CALIBRE | 51.2 mm 2.015 in | WEIGHT | 4.1/3.32 kg 9/7.3 lb |
| BARREL LENGTH | 665/481.6 mm 26.19 in/18.96 in | MAXIMUM RANGE | 456/320 m 500/350 yards |
| BORE LENGTH | 506.5/321.8 mm 19.94/12.67 in | BOMB WEIGHT (HE) | 1.02 kg 2.25 lb |

*This photograph was taken during the early days of the British Parachute Regiment in late 1942. The men are from the Royal Ulster Rifles and are using a Mark 11*** 2-inch mortar as their special Mark VII* or VIII versions had not then been made*

*Comparison between the Airborne version (left) and the Infantry version (right) of the 2-inch mortar*

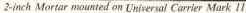

*2-inch Mortar mounted on Universal Carrier Mark 11*

# Ordnance, M.L., Mortar, 3 inch

The first 3-inch mortar, the Mark 1 entered official service in March 1917 and was the forerunner of the modern infantry mortar. After 1918 development of the 3-inch mortar was slow but sure so that in 1939 the British Army was equipped with the Mark 2 which was a much modernised version of the original Mark 1 using modern ammunition. A decision made in 1932 meant that the 3-inch mortar replaced the 3.7 inch howitzer as the standard infantry support weapon and by 1939 the change was complete. Experience in action soon showed that the Mark 2 lacked range when compared to German and Italian equipments and demands were made for design staffs to increase performance. As a result of trials and changes to the propellants used the range went up from 1600 yards to 2750 yards but this was still below that of many contemporary mortars and British troops often impressed Italian and German weapons to overcome this, especially in the Desert campaigns. The mortar itself underwent some changes—the Mark 4 featured a heavier baseplate and a new sight, the Mark 5 was a lighter version for use in the Far East (only 5000 were produced), and provisions were made on some Universal Carriers for the mortar section to carry the mortar and its ammunition in and out of action swiftly. Despite its range problems the 3-inch mortar was a popular weapon in action, but it required some form of carrying vehicle or animal to transport. It was used in all theatres of war by the troops of all the Commonwealth nations.

**Data (Mark 2)**

| | |
|---|---|
| CALIBRE | 76.2 mm 3 in |
| LENGTH OVERALL | 1295 mm 51 in |
| LENGTH OF BARREL | 1190 mm 46.85 in |
| WEIGHT IN ACTION | 57.2 kg 126 lb |
| ELEVATION | 45° to 80° |
| TRAVERSE | 11° |
| MINIMUM RANGE | 114 m 125 yards |
| MAXIMUM RANGE | 2516 m 2750 yards |
| BOMB WEIGHT (HE, smoke) | 4.54 kg 10 lb |

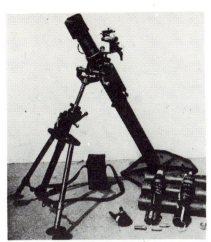

*Ordnance, M.L., Mortar, 3 inch*

*3-inch mortar in action in Germany, March 1945*

*Airborne troops practising with their 3-inch mortar in North Africa prior to the Sicilian landings in 1943*

*3-inch Mortar Mark 5 intended for airborne use and Far East service stripped ready for packing prior to dropping. The base plate was dropped separately*

*Carrier, 3-inch Mortar*

# Ordnance, S.B. 4.2-inch Mortar

The British 4.2 in mortar had its origins in a demand for a chemical mortar which was made in March 1941. At that time, firing HE rounds was considered a secondary role but in November 1941 the role was changed with HE getting the priority as a result of experience gained in North Africa. The HE round was called on to reach 4400 yards but the first bombs produced were cast iron versions which could reach only 3300 yards. A better streamlined bomb was hastily developed which reached only 4000 yards, mainly due to cast iron again being used instead of the required forged bomb for which there was insufficient manufacturing capacity. The 4.2 in mortar was usually carried in a Universal Carrier but was itself quite mobile due to its wheeled base plate. A tripod mount was used instead of the classic bipod and the design was noteworthy for the ease and speed with which a trained detachment could get the weapon in and out of action. The 4.2 in mortar was originally served by Royal Engineer units but the weapon was gradually taken over by the Royal Artillery.

**Data**

CALIBRE  106.7 mm  4.2 in
BARREL LENGTH  1730 mm  68.1 in
BORE LENGTH  1565 mm  61.6 in
WEIGHT IN ACTION  599 kg  1320 lb
ELEVATION  45° to 80°
TRAVERSE  10°
M.V.  223 m/s  731 ft/sec
MAXIMUM RANGE  3751 m  4100 yards
BOMB WEIGHT (HE)  9.08 kg  20 lb

1. *Ordnance, S.B. 4.2-inch Mortar. This photograph was taken from a German recognition manual.* 2. *A 4.2-inch mortar in action in Italy, April, 1944* 3. *A 4.2-inch mortar on the Catania Plain, Sicily, August 1943*

# U S A

**Data**
CALIBRE   60.5 mm   2.38 in
BARREL LENGTH   726 mm   28.6 in
WEIGHT IN ACTION   19.07 kg   42 lb
ELEVATION   40° to 85°
TRAVERSE   14°
MINIMUM RANGE   91 m   100 yards
MAXIMUM RANGE   1816 m   1985 yards
BOMB WEIGHT (HE)   1.36 kg   3 lb
M.V.   158 m/s   518 ft/sec

1

*1. 60mm Mortar M2—Mount M2  2. 60 mm Mortar M2 in action on Bougainville Island 3. 60 mm Mortar M2 in action in Normandy, 1944*

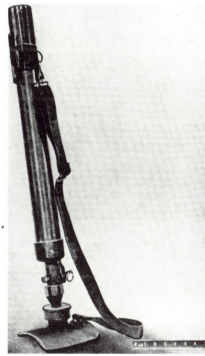

*60 mm Mortar M19—Mount M1*

*60 mm M19 on the range*

## 60 mm Mortar M2   Mount M2

In 1938 the US Ordnance board bought eight 60 mm mortars from the French Edgar Brandt firm along with a licence to build them in the USA. These eight mortars became the 60 mm Mortar M1, but the US-built version became the M2 and as such remained in production as the standard light infantry mortar for the American forces. It fired mainly HE rounds (usually the M49A2) but an extra task for this mortar was illuminating aerial targets at night for low level anti-aircraft weapons, when the M83 illuminating round was used.

2

3

## 60 mm Mortar M19   Mount M1

Originally this mortar was designated T18E6 and was a much simplified version of the M2 mortar. It dispensed with the base plate of the M2 mount and instead used a simple spade rather like that used on the British 2 in mortar. Only a few were produced as the weapon lacked accuracy and range but some were issued to airborne and special purpose units where their portability could be used to good effect. Normal 60 mm ammunition was used but only one charge, instead of the five used on the M2, propelled the bomb.

**Data**
CALIBRE   60.5 mm   2.38 in
LENGTH OVERALL   726 mm   28.6 in
WEIGHT COMPLETE   9 kg   20 lb
M.V.   89 m/s   292 ft/sec

MINIMUM RANGE   68 m   75 yards
MAXIMUM RANGE   747 m   816 yards
MAXIMUM RANGE (practical)   320 m   350 yards
BOMB WEIGHT (HE)   1.36 kg   3 lb

# 81 mm Mortar M1   Mount M1

The 81 mm M1 had its origins in a French Edgar Brandt design which was licence-built in the USA. It remained in production and service throughout the war and served on all fronts. Completely conventional in design and manufacture the 81 mm M1 fired a wide range of projectiles by using up to six charge increments. It could be carried into action by two men but special mule packs were issued and the Hand Cart M6A1 was widely used. The 81 mm M1 was also mounted on the Half-track Mortar Carrier M4 and a variety of other vehicles. As an accessory an extension tube, the T1, could be fitted to increase range but it was little used. As the war ended, a shortened version of the M1 was produced as the T27 'Universal' but few were produced.

**Data**
CALIBRE   81 mm   3.2 in
BARREL LENGTH   1257 mm   49.5 in
WEIGHT IN ACTION   61.7 kg   136 lb
ELEVATION   40° to 85°
TRAVERSE   14°
M.V. (max)   227 m/s   744 ft/sec
MINIMUM RANGE (M43A1)   91 m
  100 yards
MAXIMUM RANGE (M43A1)   3010 m
  3290 yards
BOMB WEIGHT (HE, M43A1)   3.12 kg
  6.87 lb
BOMB WEIGHT (HE, M36)   4.82 kg
  10.62 lb
BOMB WEIGHT (Chemical, M57)   4.88 kg
  10.75 lb

**Self-propelled Carriages**
T19 Mortar Carrier (M2 Half-track).
  Became M4
M4 Mortar Carrier (M2 Half-track)
M4A1 Mortar Carrier (M3 Half-track)
M21 Mortar Carrier (M3 Half-track)

*M1 in Strasbourg, November 1944, firing bombs across the Rhine into Kehl*

*81 mm Mortar M1—Mount M1*

*M1 in use in Tunisia, 1943*

*Carrier, 81 mm Mortar, Half-track, M21*

*81 mm Mortar with extension tube T1*

*An M21 in action near Amonines, Belgium, during December 1944*

## 4.2 in Chemical Mortar

**Data**

CALIBRE    107 mm    4.2 in
BARREL LENGTH    1018.7 mm    40.1 in
WEIGHT IN ACTION    149.8 kg    330 lb
MINIMUM RANGE    549 m    600 yards
MAXIMUM RANGE    4026 m    4400 yards
BOMB WEIGHT (Chemical, M4)    14.5 kg
   32 lb
BOMB WEIGHT (Chemical, M2)    11.58 kg
   25.5 lb

The American 4.2 in mortar had a lengthy gestation period before it was officially adopted as the standard weapon of the US Army's Chemical Warfare Service. Its role was supposed to be that of laying smoke screens and saturating enemy positions with gas but it was not long before an HE round was developed (1943) and after that the 4.2 in mortar was employed primarily as an infantry support weapon. It differed from other American mortars in having a rifled barrel but was still muzzle-loaded. On the move it was usually carried in a hand cart or small vehicle. In action it was invaluable in jungle warfare as it could be taken where heavier artillery could not move, but on the soft soil of many South Pacific islands the base plate had a habit of sinking into the ground when fired. This was overcome by a variety of plank and bamboo rafts placed under the plate. Some 4.2 in mortars were secured to landing craft decks and fired during the last stages of a landing. A variety of HE and chemical shells was available.

*A Chinese instructor giving instruction on the 4.2 to Chinese troops under the eye of an American instructor at Ramgarh on the China-Burma border, August 1944*

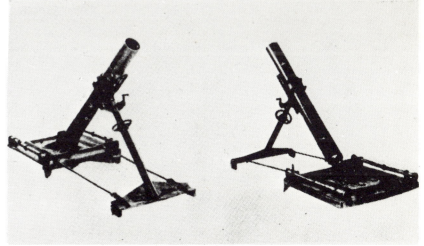

*Two views of the American 4.2-inch Chemical Mortar*

*A 4.2-inch mortar unit firing at Brest.*

*A 4.2 in action in Germany*

# 105 mm Mortar T13   Mount T12

The 105 mm Mortar appeared in 1944 and was intended to be an infantry support weapon for use immediately after the first landing on an enemy coast. Its prime function was to give covering fire until heavier artillery could be landed. By the time the first few were ready for trials the 4.2 in mortar had established itself in the role intended for the 105 mm T13 so very few were made and as soon as the war was over those few were withdrawn from service.

**Data**

| | | | | | | |
|---|---|---|---|---|---|---|
| CALIBRE | 105 mm | 4.14 in | | ELEVATION | 45° to 85° | |
| LENGTH OF BARREL | 1880 mm | 74 in | | TRAVERSE | 16° | |
| WEIGHT IN ACTION | 86.4 kg | 190.3 lb | | MAXIMUM RANGE | 3660 m | 4000 yards |
| | | | | BOMB WEIGHT | 15.9 kg | 35 lb |

*105mm Mortar T13—Mount T12*

## 155 mm Mortar T25   Mount T16E2

### Data
CALIBRE   155 mm   6.1 in
BARREL LENGTH   1828.8 mm   72 in
WEIGHT IN ACTION   259.2 kg   571 lb
ELEVATION   45° to 85°
TRAVERSE   14°
MINIMUM RANGE   183 m   200 yards
MAXIMUM RANGE   2292 m   2505 yards
BOMB WEIGHT (HE, T26E1)   28.83 kg
   63.5 lb

At the same time as the 105 mm Mortar T13 was being developed an even heavier mortar, the 155 mm T25 was being produced. This heavy weapon was intended as a heavy support weapon for use in amphibious landings and some were used on troop trials in the South West Pacific theatre during 1944. There, the shell weight was found very useful but the mortar was difficult to handle in close terrain and required a lot of digging-in. As soon as the war was over it was withdrawn from use, but not before several attempts had been made to put the piece on mobile mountings, none of which were taken into service. Construction of the T25 was conventional but the bipod was separated from the barrel by a recoil absorbing mechanism.

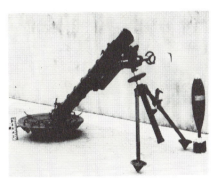

*155 mm Mortar T25—Mount T16E2*

*155 mm Mortar in action in the Pacific theatre*

# USSR

## 37 mm Spade Mortar

To this day little information exists on the Russian 37 mm Spade Mortar. It was a unique weapon that, when carried, resembled a conventional short-handled spade, but it could be quickly converted into a mortar by pulling a monopod stabilising leg out of the 'handle' which unlocked the 'spade' to form a base plate. It could function as a normal spade when folded so the basic idea may have been to give every soldier his own mortar, but the 37 mm mortar appears to have been little used. The correct Russian designation for this oddity is unknown—even the Germans were unable to discover it for they gave the weapon the reporting designation of 3.7 cm Spatengranatwerfer 161(r).

### Data
CALIBRE   37 mm   1.45 in
BARREL LENGTH   520 mm   20.47 in
BORE LENGTH   375 mm   14.76 in

WEIGHT   2.4 kg   5.3 lb
MAXIMUM RANGE (approx)   300 m
   328 yards
BOMB WEIGHT (approx)   0.68 kg   1.5 lb

*37 mm Spade Mortar ready for action*

*Spade Mortar ready for use as a spade*

# 50-PM 38

The 50 mm Model 1938 was the result of a long series of Russian experiments to produce a light infantry mortar. For its task it turned out to be rather more complicated and expensive than the production requirements demanded and it was produced in small numbers only before being replaced by the Model 1939. Its main design feature was that the barrel was clamped at two elevation angles only—45° and 75°. Range variations were made by altering a sleeve round the base of the barrel. This sleeve opened a series of gas ports which bled off exhaust gases and so determined the range. Despite the small number produced, some fell into German hands in 1941 and they were taken over as the 5 cm Granatwerfer 205/1(r).

**Data**

| | | |
|---|---|---|
| CALIBRE | 50 mm | 1.97 in |
| BARREL LENGTH | 780 mm | 30.7 in |
| BORE LENGTH | 553 mm | 21.77 in |
| WEIGHT IN ACTION | 12.1 kg | 26.6 lb |
| ELEVATION (fixed) | 45°, 75° plus 82° on some models | |
| TRAVERSE | 6° | |
| M.V. (max) | 96 m/s | 315 ft/sec |
| MAXIMUM RANGE (45°) | 800 m | 875 yards |
| MAXIMUM RANGE (75°) | 402 m | 440 yards |
| MAXIMUM RANGE (82°) | 100 m | 109 yards |
| BOMB WEIGHT | 0.85 kg | 1.875 lb |

*50-PM 38*

*A 50-PM 38 in action during the Winter of 1942-1943*

# 50-PM 39

The 50 mm Model 1939 was intended to replace the Model 1938 as it had proved expensive to produce. As things turned out the Model 1939 was itself replaced very quickly by an even cheaper version, the Model 1940. The Model 1939 at first glance seemed identical to the Model 1938 but the gas vents were omitted in favour of the usual elevation controls on the bipod. The Model 1939 retained the Model 1938 base plate and sight. In German use the Model 1939 became the 5 cm Granatwerfer 205/2(r).

**Data**

| | | |
|---|---|---|
| CALIBRE | 50 mm | 1.97 in |
| BARREL LENGTH | 775 mm | 30.5 in |
| BORE LENGTH | 545 mm | 21.46 in |
| WEIGHT IN ACTION | 16.98 kg | 37.4 lb |
| ELEVATION | 45° to 85° | |
| TRAVERSE | 7° | |
| M.V. (max) | 96 m/s | 315 ft/sec |
| MAXIMUM RANGE | 800 m | 875 yards |
| BOMB WEIGHT | 0.85 kg | 1.875 lb |

*50-PM 39*

## Data

CALIBRE   50 mm   1.97 in
BARREL LENGTH   630 mm   24.8 in
BORE LENGTH   533 mm   20.98 in
WEIGHT IN ACTION   9.3 kg   20.5 lb
ELEVATION (fixed)   45°, 75°
TRAVERSE   9° at 45°, 16° at 75°
MAXIMUM RANGE (45°)   800 m   875 yards
MAXIMUM RANGE (75°)   402 m   440 yards
BOMB WEIGHT   0.85 kg   1.875 lb

*50-PM 40*

## Data

CALIBRE   50 mm   1.97 in
BARREL LENGTH   610 mm   24 in
BORE LENGTH   559 mm   22 in
WEIGHT IN ACTION   10.05 kg   22.2 lb
ELEVATION (fixed)   45°, 75°
TRAVERSE   9° at 45°, 16° at 75°
M.V. (max)   86 m/s   315 ft/sec
MAXIMUM RANGE (45°)   800 m   875 yards
MAXIMUM RANGE (75°)   402 m   440 yards
BOMB WEIGHT   0.85 kg   1.875 lb

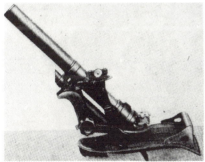

*50-PM 41*

# 50-PM 40

The 50 mm Model 1940 was produced in large numbers and it was a popular and effective weapon that could be easily and cheaply produced as its base plate and bipod were simple steel stampings. The barrel reverted to the two fixed elevation angles as on the Model 1938 and again range variation was brought about by gas vents. The bipod was further simplified by incorporating a novel and simple method of cross-levelling for laying which was so successful it was used on later and heavier mortars. Trials were carried out using three barrels on one Model 1940 base plate and bipod which were intended to be fired together but the experiment was not a success. The Model 1940 was used widely and any that fell into German hands were turned against their former owners as the 5 cm Granatwerfer 205/3(r).

# 50-PM 41

With the 50 mm Model 1941 the Russian light mortars went one stage further in the search for simplicity and cheap manufacture. The Model 1941 dispensed with a bipod and used a barrel yoke which incorporated all the traverse and cross-levelling controls. Elevation angles remained fixed at 45° and 75° but exhaust gases were vented forward through a tube under the muzzle. The sight was simplified also. The ammunition remained the same as for the earlier models and continued to be propelled by a single charge with no increments. Oddly enough, no records exist of this mortar being used by the Germans, but they gave it the reporting designation of 5 cm Granatwerfer 200(r).

*50-PM 41 on parade*

# 82-PM 36

The 82 mm Model was a Russian copy of the French Brandt 81 mm mortar and, apart from the slight increase in calibre was identical to it in all respects. Having said that there is little else to remark on the Model 1936 except that it was in widespread use in 1941. As usual, the Germans used as much captured equipment as they could and so the Model 1936 became the 8.2 cm Granatwerfer 274/1(r). German 8.1 cm ammunition could be fired from the Russian 82 mm mortars but accuracy suffered as a result.

**Data**
CALIBRE  82 mm  3.228 in
BARREL LENGTH  1320 mm  51.97 in
BORE LENGTH  1225 mm  48.23 in
WEIGHT IN ACTION  62 kg  136.7 lb
ELEVATION  45° to 85°
TRAVERSE  6° to 11°—variable with elevation
M.V.  202 m/s  663 ft/sec
MAXIMUM RANGE  3000 m  3282 yards
BOMB WEIGHT  3.35 kg  7.4 lb
BOMB WEIGHT  3.4 kg  7.5 lb

*The crew of an 82-PM 36 advancing on the Voronezh Front, August 1943*

82-PM 36

*82-PM 36 mortars in action in the Ukraine, late 1943. These mortars were carried into action on motor-cycle combinations*

82-PM 36 in action, 1943

# 82-PM 37

The basic French design of the 82 mm Model 1936 was revised in 1937 to produce the 82 mm Model 1937. Several changes were made, one of which was the addition of recoil springs between the barrel and bipod to reduce stress on the bipod and reduce the amount of re-laying during a long 'shoot'. The traverse controls were altered slightly but the main change was made to the base plate which became circular—however a small rectangular plate was used by mountain units. This circular base plate became one of the main recognition points of Russian mortars. In German hands the Model 1937 became the 8.2 cm Granatwerfer 274/2(r).

**Data**
CALIBRE  82 mm  3.228 in
BARREL LENGTH  1320 mm  51.97 in
BORE LENGTH  1225 mm  48.23 in
WEIGHT IN ACTION  57.34 kg  126.3 lb
ELEVATION  45° to 85°
TRAVERSE  6° to 11°—variable with
  elevation
M.V.  202 m/s  663 ft/sec
MAXIMUM RANGE  3100 m  3391 yards
BOMB WEIGHT  3.35 kg  7.4 lb
BOMB WEIGHT  3.4 kg  7.5 lb

*82-PM 37*

*The simple open sight used on the 82-PM 37*

# 82-PM 41

In 1941 the Russians produced their 82 mm Model 1941 mortar which differed from earlier models in having a new bipod design. This new bipod was produced to increase the tactical mobility of the 82 mm mortar. In 1941 transport vehicles were in short supply in Russia so the new model was designed for hand-towing. Stamped steel wheels could be fitted over stub axles on the bipod legs after the bipod had been secured against the base plate. A handle attachment was fitted over the muzzle and the mortar could then be towed by one or two men. This version was used by the Germans as the 8.2 cm Granatwerfer 274/3(r). In 1943 the idea was taken a stage further by making the wheels a permanent fixture on the bipod. In action they were above the bipod feet and only became effective when the bipod was folded back. This version was the 82 mm Model 1943 or 82-PM 43, and it remained in use for many years.

*82-PM 41*

**Data (Model 1941)**

| | | | |
|---|---|---|---|
| CALIBRE | 82 mm 3.228 in | TRAVERSE | 5° to 10°—variable with elevation |
| BARREL LENGTH | 1320 mm 51.97 in | M.V. | 202 m/s 663 ft/sec |
| BORE LENGTH | 1225 mm 48.23 in | MAXIMUM RANGE | 3100 m 3391 yards |
| WEIGHT IN ACTION | 45 kg 99.2 lb | BOMB WEIGHT | 3.35 kg 7.4 lb |
| ELEVATION | 45° to 85° | BOMB WEIGHT | 3.4 kg 7.5 lb |

*82-PM 41 on parade*

*82-PM 41 ready for towing*

*An 82-PM 41 detachment posing for the camera, July 1942*

*82-PM 43*

# 107-PBHM 38

**Data**

CALIBRE 107 mm 4.21 in
BARREL LENGTH 1570 mm 61.8 in
BORE LENGTH 1400 mm 55.12 in
WEIGHT IN ACTION 170.7 kg 376 lb
WEIGHT TRAVELLING 850 kg 1874 lb
ELEVATION 45° to 80°
TRAVERSE 6°
M.V. 302 m/s 990 ft/sec
MAXIMUM RANGE 6314 m 6900 yards
BOMB WEIGHT 8 kg 17.64 lb

The 107 mm Mountain Mortar Model 1938 was a scaled-up version of the 82 mm Model 1937 produced especially for Russian mountain units. It featured a light tubular steel limber onto which the mortar could be folded for horse or vehicle towing—this limber was incorporated into the 120 mm Mortar Model 1938. For transport over rough ground the mortar could be broken down for pack carrying. Firing could be by either gravity percussion or by a trigger. The ammunition was fired by a single primary cartridge and up to four increments—the rounds could be one of two types of HE, smoke, incendiary or chemical. Any that were captured by the Germans were used by them as the 10.7 cm Gebirgsgranatwerfer 328(r).

*107-PBHM 38*

*107-PBHM 38 in use on the Northern Front, March 1942*

31

# 120-HM 38

Like the 107 mm Model 1938, the 120 mm Regimental Mortar Model 1938 was a scaled-up version of the 82 mm Model 1937. It used the same two-wheeled limber as the 107 mm Model 1938 but this was usually allied to a two-wheeled ammunition cart to which it was attached for towing—this cart carried 20 rounds. By all accounts, the 120 mm Model 1938 can be assessed as one of the best mortar designs of the war. It fired a heavy bomb with a good warhead, it was highly mobile and could be taken in and out of action very quickly, and it had a most useful range. The Germans paid the design the compliment of not only taking it into service as the 12 cm Granatwerfer 378(r) but of copying the design and manufacturing it as the 12 cm Granatwerfer 42.

The later 120-HM 43 was essentially similar to the Model 1938 but used a single shock absorber on the barrel-bipod mounting.

**Data**
CALIBRE   120 mm   4.72 in
BARREL LENGTH (L/15.5)   1862 mm   73.3 in
BORE LENGTH   1536 mm   60.47 in
WEIGHT IN ACTION   280.1 kg   617 lb
WEIGHT TRAVELLING   477.6 kg   1052 lb
ELEVATION   45° to 80°
TRAVERSE   6°
M.V.   272 m/s   892 ft/sec
MAXIMUM RANGE   6000 m   6564 yards
BOMB WEIGHT (HE)   16 kg   35.3 lb

*120-HM 38*

*120-HM 38 ready for towing*

*A section of 120-HM 38s in action in the Kuban Valley*

120-HM 43

120-HM 38 in action in the Caucasian Hills, September 1942

# 160 mm Mortar Model 1943

The effectiveness of the Russian 120 mm mortar was such that the Russians went one step upwards in calibre and produced a 160 mm mortar in 1943. This became the 160 mm Mortar Model 1943 although it more closely resembled a light artillery piece than a mortar. It did use a smooth-bored barrel but it was breech-loaded and trigger-fired. Used by divisional artillery units it was a powerful and useful weapon.

**Data**
CALIBRE   160 mm   6.3 in
BARREL LENGTH   2896 mm   114 in
WEIGHT IN ACTION   1080.5 kg   2380 lb
ELEVATION (max)   50°
TRAVERSE   17°
M.V.   305 m/s   1000 ft/sec
MINIMUM RANGE   750 m   820 yards
MAXIMUM RANGE
BOMB WEIGHT (HE)   41.14 kg   90.17 kg

160 mm Mortar Model 1943

# Rockets

## GERMANY

*7.3 cm Propagandagranate 41*

## 7.3 cm Propagandagranate 41

Perhaps the most specialised and unusual role the rocket was called on to perform during World War 2 was that of distributing propaganda leaflets. This role was quite a familiar one for artillery but when the Germans produced the 7.3 cm Propagandagranate 41 in 1941 they produced another remarkable 'first'. The Propagandagranate 41 (or Propagandageschoss) was a simple spin-stabilised rocket containing about 0.5 lb of leaflets wrapped round a spring. When fired singly from the Propagandawerfer 41 launcher the rocket motor ignited a delay chain. After a set time the chain ignited a small bursting charge which blew apart the sides of the payload chamber—the spring then opened and scattered the leaflets.

**Data**
OVERALL LENGTH   409 mm   16.1 in
LENGTH OF MESSAGE BODY   174.5 mm   6.87 in
MAXIMUM DIAMETER   72.4 mm   2.85 in
WEIGHT   3.24 kg   7.125 lb
WEIGHT OF PROPELLANT   0.48 kg   1.0625 lb
WEIGHT OF PAYLOAD   0.23 kg   0.5 lb

**Launcher**
7.3 cm Propagandawerfer 41

## 7.3 cm Raketen Sprenggranate

Designed to be fired in salvoes against low-flying aircraft, the 7.3 cm Raketen Sprenggranate was a simple spin-stabilised unguided rocket projectile that entered service in late 1944. The warhead used a nose percussion fuze (the Raketenaufschlagzünder 51, or RaZ 51) but incorporated a timed self-igniting device for safety in the case of a miss. There were two possible fillings for the warhead, both being basically RDX/TNT sticks weighing 0.28 kg. The propellant was a single ribbed stick charge which was percussion ignited

**Data**
OVERALL LENGTH   281.7 mm   11.09 in
MAXIMUM DIAMETER   72.9 mm   2.87 in
WEIGHT   2.74 kg   6 lb
WEIGHT OF PROPELLANT   0.48 kg   1.0625 lb
WEIGHT OF EXPLOSIVE   0.28 kg   0.62 lb

**Launchers**
Föhn Gerat
7.5 cm Multiple Fortress Rocket Launcher
  (Allied designation)

## 7.3 cm Propagandawerfer 41

The most specialised German rocket launcher was the little 7.3 cm Propagandawerfer 41 which was used by specially-trained propaganda troops to fire the 7.3 cm Propagandagranate 41 leaflet rocket. The launcher consisted of a steel tube frame upon which was mounted a steel rail trough at the top of which was placed the rocket ready to be fired. It was held there until released by a lanyard when it fell down the trough until the base hit a striker pin. This pin set off the rocket which was launched along the rails. The launcher was carried by one man when on the move. Very few of these rather expensive leaflet launchers appear to have been produced or used.

**Data**
LENGTH OF GUIDE RAILS   749 mm   29.5 in
LENGTH OVERALL   1161 mm   45.7 in
WIDTH OVERALL   500 mm   19.7 in
ELEVATION (fixed)   45°
WEIGHT   12.26 kg   27 lb

## 7.3 cm Föhn Gerät

The true designation of the device that has become known as the Föhn Gerät is not known for the name Föhn was a cover code name only. It was a launcher for the 7.3 cm HE rockets and was intended primarily for anti-aircraft use. In practice it was often emplaced to cover river crossings as well. It was a conventional box launcher that could fire thirty-five rockets which were loaded in five horizontal and seven vertical rows. The launchers were either emplaced in concrete or mounted on a sheet steel base. A 360° mount could be elevated by a layer situated in a steel box on the left inside which were the controls and sights which were so simple that it reasonable to assume that this equipment was intended only for use against low-flying aircraft. Rockets could be fired only in a single salvo.

*Static version of Föhn Gerat*

**Data**
LENGTH OF RAILS   787 mm   31 in
HEIGHT OF BOX   813 mm   32 in
WIDTH OF BOX   584 mm   23 in
ELEVATION   −10° to +90°
TRAVERSE   360°

# 8 cm Raketen Sprenggranate

**Data**
OVERALL LENGTH   724 mm   28.5 in
BODY DIAMETER   78 mm   3.07 in
WEIGHT   6.9 kg   15.19 lb
WEIGHT OF PROPELLANT   1.965 kg
  4.328 lb
WEIGHT OF EXPLOSIVE   0.608 kg   1.34 lb
M.V.   290 m/s   950 ft/sec
RANGE   5300 m   5798 yards

**Launchers**
Mantlerohr
8 cm R-Vielfachwerfer

Soon after the Germans attacked Russia they came up against the Russian Katyusha rockets which had a profound effect on the Germans on the receiving end. It was not long before a proposal was made to copy the Russian rocket but there was little manufacturing capacity spare at the time. This did not deter the members of the Waffen SS from using their party influence to get the rockets made, and thus the result, the 8 cm Raketen Sprenggranate, became a weapon used almost exclusively by SS formations. In many ways it was a much simpler device than the other German rockets. Being fin-stabilised it did not need the expensive machining that was needed on the venturii of spin-stabilised rockets. Another important feature was that the motor used cordite sticks instead of expensive and increasingly scarce double-based propellants. As always the SS made much political capital out of these facts in their internal squabbles with the regular Wehrmacht. There was little remarkable about the basic design save the arming device which was set off by the rocket motor itself—heat melted a soft metal ring which allowed the percussion detonator to move into the armed state ready for a contact detonation. A smoke carrying version of the 8 cm rocket was reported but no records can be found.

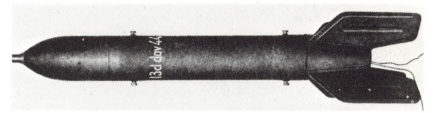

*8 cm Raketen Sprenggranate*

# 8 cm R-Vielfachwerfer

**Data**
WEIGHT IN ACTION (2 salvoes on vehicle)
  6853 kg   15,111 lb
WEIGHT WITHOUT AMMUNITION   6200 kg
  13,671 lb

ELEVATION   0° to + 37°
TRAVERSE   360°

Very little data remain of the launchers intended for use with the 8 cm rockets used by the Waffen-SS. One, known as the Mantlerohr, was a single round launcher which fired the rocket from a barrel but no known data or illustrations have survived. Another, the 8 cm R-Vielfachwerfer, was a multiple rail launcher which fired either twenty-four or forty-eight round salvoes. It was mounted on a captured French Somua half-track but it seems very likely that other vehicles were used. The data refers to the Somua vehicle.

*Close-up of 8 cm R-Vielfachwerfer on Somua half-track*

# 8.6 cm Raketen Sprenggranate L/4.8

**Data**
LENGTH OVERALL   412.8 mm   16.25 in
BODY WIDTH   86 mm   3.38 in
WEIGHT   8.15 kg   17.94 lb
WEIGHT OF PROPELLANT   1.14 kg   2.5 lb
MAXIMUM HEIGHT (90°)   2440 m   8000 ft

There were three versions of the 8.6 cm R.Spreng.—the /400, /600 and /800 which differed only in the delay train which set off the main charge. In addition, the /400 and /800 had contact fuzes. All versions were intended for use as anti-aircraft rockets and started life as naval projectiles, but they were also used as land-based projectiles. Like most other German rockets all three were spin-stabilised.

# 8.8 cm Raketenpanzerbüchse Grenate 4322 und 4992

The 8.8 cm rocket grenades were intended as anti-tank projectiles. Their basic design was based on the American 2.36 in Rocket M6, examples of which had been captured in Tunisia in 1943. The first German example was the 8.8 cm RPzBGr 4322 designed to be fired from the 8.8 cm RP 43. Its main feature was the tank-killing hollow-charge head set off by a nose percussion fuze. The rocket motor was made up of seven propellant sticks ignited by a small electrical charge. Range of the 4322 was a maximum of 165 yards but it could penetrate up to 8.25 in of tank armour. Guidance was by drum fins. The later RPzBGr 4992 was similar in most details but had a greater range of 220 yards. As the propellant used in these grenades was very prone to temperature effects special batches had to be produced for use in extremes of hot and cold climate.

**Data**

LENGTH OVERALL   649 mm   25.56 in
BODY DIAMETER   87.3 mm   3.437 in
WEIGHT   3.3 kg   7.26 lb
WEIGHT OF PROPELLANT   0.183 kg   0.403 lb
WEIGHT OF EXPLOSIVE   0.667 kg   1.47 lb
M.V. (4322)   104 m/s   340 ft/sec
MAXIMUM RANGE (4322)   151 m   165 yards
MAXIMUM RANGE (4992)   201 m   220 yards

**Launchers**
Raketenpanzerbüchse 43 (4322 only)
Raketenpanzerbüchse 54 (4322 only)
Raketenpanzerbüchse 54/1 (4322 and 4992)

*8.8 cm Racketenpanzerbüchse Granate 4322*

*RP43*

# 8.8 cm Racketenpanzerbüchse Granate 4312

Although the basic design of the RPzBGr 4312 was similar to that of the 4322 and 4992 it differed in several ways. It used a percussion igniter and the rocket motor was much smaller (a single stick instead of seven). As a result it was shorter than the two rockets intended for use with the shoulder-mounted launchers, but it could be fired further as it was intended for use with the 8.8 cm Raketenwerfer 43. The warhead remained the same as that on the 4322.

**Data**

LENGTH OVERALL   498.8 mm   19.64 in
BODY DIAMETER   88.7 mm   3.492 in
WEIGHT   2.66 kg   5.85 lb
WEIGHT OF PROPELLANT   0.046 kg
   0.102 lb
WEIGHT OF EXPLOSIVE   0.656 kg   1.446 lb
M.V.   140 m/s   459 ft/sec
MAXIMUM RANGE   700 m   766 yards

**Launcher**
8.8 cm Raketenwerfer 43

*8.8 cm Racketenwerfer 43*

# 15 cm Wurfgranate 41 Spreng

Probably the most frequently encountered German artillery rocket was the 15 cm Wgr 41 Spr, an HE projectile. Fired from the numerous 15 cm rocket launchers its distinctive droning sound gave rise to the 'Moaning Minnie' nickname bestowed upon it by the Allies. It first entered service in 1942 and was unique among German rockets in having its explosive warhead behind the rocket motor. The motor exhausts were about two-thirds of the way down the body in a ring of 26 angled veturi to give spin stabilisation. Just behind the venturi was a base canister holding the warhead. This configuration was chosen to ensure that the rocket motor and casing would be added to the warheads explosive effects—in conventional rockets the motor tended to fly off in one piece. The motor consisted of seven diethylene glycol dinitrate sticks which were ignited from a cellulose stick. This stick was ignited electrically by an ERZ 39 initiator. Special rounds were issued for tropical and arctic use. Rounds were delivered to the front in individual wooden boxes.

**Data**

LENGTH OVERALL   979 mm   38.55 in
DIAMETER   158 mm   6.22 in
WEIGHT   31.8 kg   70 lb
WEIGHT OF PROPELLANT   6.35 kg   14 lb
WEIGHT OF EXPLOSIVE   2.5 kg   5.5 lb
M.V.   342 m/s   1120 ft/sec
MAXIMUM RANGE   7066 m   7723 yards

**Launchers**
15 cm Nebelwerfer 41
15 cm Do-gerät 38
15 cm Panzerwerfer 42
30 cm Raketenwerfer 56

*15 cm Wurfgranate 41 Spreng*

## Data

LENGTH OVERALL  1020 mm  40.16 in
DIAMETER  158 mm  6.22 in
WEIGHT  35.9 kg  79 lb
WEIGHT OF PROPELLANT  6.35 kg  14 lb
WEIGHT OF FILLING  3.86 kg  8.5 lb
M.V.  342 m/s  1120 ft/sec
MAXIMUM RANGE  6905 m  7546 yards

**Launchers**
As 15 cm Wgr 41 Spr

## Data

BARREL INTERNAL DIAMETER  158.5 mm
  6.24 in
BARREL LENGTH  1300 mm  51.2 in
WEIGHT IN ACTION LOADED  770 kg
  1697.85 lb
WEIGHT IN ACTION EMPTY  510 kg
  1124.55 lb
WIDTH ON TOW  1660 mm  65.54 in
LENGTH ON TOW  3600 mm  141.7 in
HEIGHT ON TOW  1400 mm  55.12 in
TRACK  1430 mm  56.3 in
ELEVATION  5° to 45°
TRAVERSE  27°

# 15 cm Wurfgranate 41 w Kh Nebel

The smoke-producing 15 cm rocket followed the same general design as the 15 cm HE round, and differed only in dimensions and weights. The same dimensions also applied to the rockets intended to carry chemical or gas fillings. One of these rockets was the 15 cm Wgr 41 Grunring and another the 15 cm Wgr 41 w Kh Farbring, but they were not used during the war.

# 15 cm Nebelwerfer 41

The 15 cm Nebelwerfer 41 was the result of a great deal of experimental work devoted to producing a viable field artillery rocket launcher. It first appeared in 1941 and went into large-scale action in 1942. In time it became the standard launcher for the Werferabteilung and served on all fronts. The Nebelwerfer 41 was a simple, six-barrelled launcher that used the same carriage as the 3.7 cm Pak 35/36 with a simple sighting system. The rockets were fired singly at two-second intervals by one of the four-man crew using a small electrical generator. As the rockets were fired the crew had to take cover some ten yards away, for the rocket back-blast was considerable and threw up clouds of dust and debris. The rockets themselves made a distinctive droning sound in flight which led to them being called the 'Moaning Minnies' by the Allies. On the move the Nebelwerfer was towed by a SdKfz 11/1, but many other towing vehicles were used including horses on occasion.

*15 cm Nebelwerfer 41*

*Manhandling a 15 cm NbW 41 onto a SdKfz 11 tractor*

# 15 cm Panzerwerfer 42

One of the main disadvantages of the towed Nebelwerfer 41 was that when fired it produced large clouds of dust and debris while the rockets themselves left conspicuous smoke trails. Thus the Nebelwerfer batteries soon found themselves subjected to counter-battery fire and often were immobilised or had to withdraw. When working with Panzer units the towed Nebelwerfer batteries had difficulty in keeping up with them so the answer to these tactical problems was to make the rocket projectors more mobile. The result was the ten-barrel Panzerwerfer 42 mounted on the armoured SdKfz 4/1 Maultier half-track. The barrels were the same as used on the Nebelwerfer 41 arranged in two rows of five. Loading had to be carried out outside the armoured cab but the crew could retire inside for firing. The Maultier units were widely used on all fronts. In 1944 some Panzerwerfer 42s were fitted to armoured Schwerer Wehrmachtschlepper (SWS) half-tracks. The Maultier could carry ten rounds internally and the SWS twenty-six.

**Data**

BARREL INTERNAL DIAMETER   158.5 mm
6.24 in
BARREL LENGTH   1300 mm   51.24 in
WEIGHT OF PROJECTOR   800 kg   1764 lb
ELEVATION   0° to +80°
TRAVERSE   270°

*15 cm Panzerwerfer 42 (SdKfz 4/1) 'Opel Maultier'*

*Panzerwerfer 42 in action*

*15 cm PzW 42 on a Schwerer Wehrmacht- schlepper (SWS)*

# 15 cm Scheinsignalraketen

The 15 cm Schneinsignalraketen, or SSR, was no relation of the 15 cm field rockets but was a specialised fin-stabilised rocket which fired large signal flares, usually at night, as an aid to navigation for night fighters. Very little information seems to survive about this projectile but they came into use during late 1943. They were fired direct from their crates which had folding legs that converted the crate into a firing stand. These crates, when folded, were 1970 mm long, 370 mm wide and 330 mm high. Complete with the rocket they weighed 53 kg (116.9 lb). There were various alternative fillings for the rockets including one illuminating round which was intended to illuminate aircraft for the benefit of "Wilde-Sau' night fighters that fought without radar aids. The rocket without a pyrotechnic warhead weighed 30 kg (66.15 lb) and the warheads weighed either 12 or 13 kg (26.5 or 28.6 lb).

## 21 cm Wurfgranate 42 Spreng

**Data**

LENGTH OVERALL   1249.9 mm   49.21 in
BODY DIAMETER   210 mm   8.27 in
WEIGHT   109.55 kg   241.3 lb
WEIGHT OF PROPELLANT   18.27 kg   40.25 lb
WEIGHT OF EXPLOSIVE   10.17 kg   22.4 lb

**Launcher**
21 cm Nebelwerfer 42

At first glance the 21 cm Wurfgranate 42 resembled a conventional artillery shell for considerable trouble had been taken by the designers to reduce drag and thus increase range. The streamlined nose was hollow with the warhead proper behind it. The rocket motor vented from 22 venturii, angled as usual to impart spin for stabilisation in flight, and was made up of seven sticks of propellant. Captured 21 cm rockets that were taken to the USA were closely copied to produce the 210 mm T36 —these were used extensively for trials and research purposes.

*21 cm Wurfgranate 42 Spreng*

## 21 cm Nebelwerfer 42

**Data**

BARREL INTERNAL DIAMETER   214.5 mm
   8.45 in
BARREL LENGTH   1300 mm   51.2 in
WEIGHT IN ACTION LOADED   1100 kg
   2425.5 lb
WEIGHT IN ACTION EMPTY   550 kg
   1212.8 lb
WIDTH ON TOW   1660 mm   65.54 in
LENGTH ON TOW   3600 mm   141.7 in
HEIGHT ON TOW   1500 mm   59 in
TRACK   1430 mm   56.3 in
ELEVATION   −5° to +45°
TRAVERSE   24°

A most unusual example of a German attempt to produce some measure of inter-changeability and maximum utilisation of manufacturing resources was the 21 cm Nebelwerfer 42. Although the projector barrels were larger, the whole equipment was virtually the same as the 15 cm Nebelwerfer 41. It used the same carriage, towing vehicles and sights and also used a four-man crew. The first Nebelwerfer 42s entered service in 1943 although an earlier version with six barrels had been used for troop trials. The results of those trials showed that a five barrel configuration was preferable for handling purposes. This projector could fire a 21 cm rocket to a maximum of 10,000 yards (9,150 m).

*21 cm Nebelwerfer 42 with firing cable*

# 28 cm Wurfkörper Spreng

The 28 cm Wurfkörper Spreng was the first of the German rockets to see widespread service and appeared in late 1940. Its ballistic shape was poor, it had a very limited range and was clumsy and awkward to handle but it had a very heavy warhead and remained in use until 1945. The warhead contained 110 lb of amatol or TNT and was thus very useful for demolishing strongpoints, but accuracy was not of a high order. The motor was a single propellant stick venting through 26 base venturii angled to impart spin. A nose fuse was centrifugally armed. Special sealed rounds were issued for 'tropical' use. In action the 28 cm rocket could be fired from a variety of launchers but it could also be fired from its carrying crate, or 'Packkiste'.

**Data**
LENGTH OVERALL    1190 mm    46.41 in
BODY WIDTH    280 mm    11.02 in
WEIGHT    82.2 kg    181 lb
WEIGHT OF PROPELLANT    6.6 kg    14.56 lb
WEIGHT OF EXPLOSIVE    49.9 kg    110 lb
MAXIMUM RANGE    2138 m    2337 ♣

**Launchers**
Schweres Wurfgerät 40
Schweres Wurfgerät 41
28/32 cm Nebelwerfer 41
Schweres Wurfrahmen 40

*28 cm Wurfkörper Spreng in its 'Packkisste'*

# 32 cm Wurfkörper M Fl 50

The 32 cm incendiary rocket used the same rocket motor as the 28 cm HE rocket and the two shared the same launchers. They entered service at the same time and both were issued to units equipped to handle the launching systems, usually in a ratio of one incendiary to five HE. The filling in the enlarged head was a mobile mixture of petrol and diesel oil, although kerosene was sometimes used. On contact with the target the mixture was set off by a magnesium fuse. The volume of the incendiary mixture was about 11 gallons.

**Data**
LENGTH OVERALL    1289 mm    50.75 in
BODY DIAMETER    320 mm    12.6 in
WEIGHT    79 kg    174 lb
WEIGHT OF PROPELLANT    6.6 kg    14.56 lb

WEIGHT OF FILLING    39.8 kg    87.69 lb
MAXIMUM RANGE    2028 m    2217 yards

**Launchers**
As 28 cm Wurfkörper Spreng

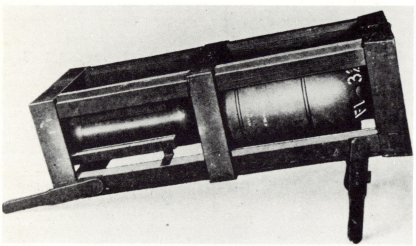

*32 cm Wurfkörper M Fl 50 in its 'Packkiste' ready to fire*

# Schweres Wurfgerät 40 und 41

**Data**

WEIGHT EMPTY (40/41) 52/110 kg
114.7/242.5 lb

WEIGHT LOADED (28 cm) (40/41) 500/558 kg
1102.5/1230.4 lb

*Schweres Wurfgerät 40*

The simplest of all the German rocket launchers were the Schweres Wurfgerät 40 and 41. Originally they were intended for use with the 28 and 32 cm rockets but later they were also used as the launcher for the 30 cm rocket. They were almost identical in appearance and the only difference between the two was that the 40 was made of wood and the 41 of steel tubing. Both could take up to four rockets in their carrying crates which acted as the guide component, as the function of the Schweres Wurfgerät was to act as an elevation support only. When the crates containing the rockets were loaded onto the frame it was elevated to the required angle and connections made to the rocket bases. The rockets were then fired in sequence electrically. In action the 40 and 41 were used to fire pre-planned barrages and were often emplaced in advance until required.

*Schweres Wurfgerät 41*

*Loading a sWG 41 ready for action in a Russian city*

# 28/32 cm Nebelwerfer 41

Designed to give more mobility than could be obtained by the static Schweres Wurfgerät 40 and 41 the 28/32 cm Nebelwerfer was a simple two-wheeled trailer upon which was mounted six launcher frames in two superimposed rows of three. The frames were contoured for the 32 cm rocket, but liner rails were provided for insertion into the frames for 28 cm rounds. Simple and relatively cheap to produce and use, the Nebelwerfer 41 became one of the mainstays of the Werferabteilung.

**Data**

WEIGHT IN ACTION LOADED (28 cm) 1630 kg
3594 lb

WEIGHT IN ACTION LOADED (32 cm) 1600 kg
3528 lb

WEIGHT EMPTY 1130 kg 2491 lb

WIDTH 1910 mm 75.2 in
LENGTH 3200 mm 126 in
HEIGHT 1690 mm 66.5 in
WHEEL TRACK 1580 mm 62.2 in
ELEVATION 0° to 45°
TRAVERSE 30°

*28/32 cm Nebelwerfer 41*

# Schwerer Wurfrahmen 40

An early and most successful attempt to increase the mobility of the heavy 28/32 cm rockets was the Schwerer Wurfrahmen 40. This was a special steel tube frame intended for fitting over a standard SdKfz 251 half-track which converted the vehicle into the SdKfz 251/1. The frames were produced by J. Gast KG of Berlin-Lichtenberg. They were intended to carry the 28/32 cm rockets in their 'Packkiste' on swivelling plates mounted on the frames at the sides of the vehicle. Each frame could be elevated seperately to alter the range and each frame was fired individually. Normally the rockets were carried inside the vehicle and loaded onto the frames only when needed. The elevation was then set and traverse was bought about simply by aiming the vehicle toward the target. The half-track/rocket combination soon became a very effective weapon and earned the nick-name of 'Stuka zum fuss'. It was encountered on all fronts throughout the war. A simplified version of the Schwerer Wurfrahmen was fittted to the little Infantrie Schlepper UE(f) which carried four rockets over the rear of the French-designed tankette. Wurfrahmen were also fitted to the sides of the Gepanzerter Munitionsschlepper UE(f), a similar vehicle to the latter, and also to the PzKpfw 35H(f)—the French Hotchkiss H35 tank. All three of these vehicles carried only four rockets instead of the normal six on the SdKfz 251/1, and were improvisations produced during 1944 to bolster anti-invasion defences in France. Although intended for use with 28/32 cm rockets, the Schwerer Wurfrahmen 40 could also be used to launch 30 cm rounds.

*SdKfz 251/1 in action in  Russia*

*SdKfz 251/1*

# 30 cm Wurfkörper 42 Spreng

The 30 cm Wurfkörper 42 Spreng (sometimes referred to as the Wurfkörper Spreng 4491) was the last and most improved of all the German field rockets to enter service. It had a vastly improved aerodynamic shape when compared to the bulbous 28 cm rockets and it had a higher payload/propellant ratio than any other field rocket. What really mattered to the men in the field was that it produced very little smoke when fired so concealment was easier. The motor was virtually an enlarged 15 cm rocket with seven propellant sticks venting through 18 venturii.

**Data**
LENGTH OVERALL   1230 mm   48.44 in
BODY DIAMETER   300 mm   11.8 in
WEIGHT   125.7 kg   277 lb
WEIGHT OF PROPELLANT   15 kg   33.234 lb
WEIGHT OF EXPLOSIVE   44.66 kg   98.375 lb
MAXIMUM RANGE   6000 m   6564 yards

**Launchers**
30 cm Nebelwerfer 42
30 cm Raketenwerfer 56

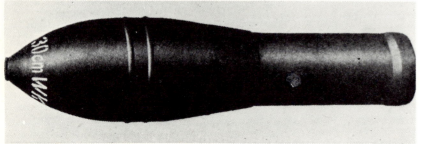

*30 cm Wurfkörper 42 Spreng*

# 30 cm Nebelwerfer 42

**Data**
WEIGHT IN ACTION (LOADED) 1144 kg
 2520 lb
WIDTH 1910 mm 75.2 in
LENGTH 3200 mm 126 in
HEIGHT 1670 mm 65.75 in
WHEEL TRACK 1580 mm 62.2 in
ELEVATION 0° to 45°
TRAVERSE 30°

This projector was simply a version of the 28/32 cm Nebelwerfer 42 intended for use with 30 cm rockets. The only change from the 28/32 cm version was that the launcher rails were recontoured to take the shape of the 30 cm round. It entered service in 1943.

*30 cm Nebelwerfer 42*

# 30 cm Raketenwerfer 56

In an attempt to utilise manufacturing facilities to the full, the 30 cm Raketenwerfer 56 used the same carriage of the 5 cm Pak 38 together with the projector frames of the 30 cm Nebelwerfer 42. The Raketenwerfer 56 could also fire the 15 cm rockets. For this purpose special liner rails were provided, and when not in use were stacked on top of the frames. One other extra was a towing eye on the axle opposite the split trails which enabled one towing vehicle to pull a string of projectors. The Raketenwerfer 56 entered service in 1944.

**Data**
PROJECTOR FRAME LENGTH 777 mm 30.6 in
PROJECTOR FRAME WIDTH 691 mm 27.2 in
PROJECTOR FRAME HEIGHT 455 mm 17.9 in
LENGTH TRAVELLING 2133 mm 84 in
WIDTH 1257 mm 49.5 in
HEIGHT 1054 mm 41.5 in
TRAIL SPREAD 1422 mm 56 in
ELEVATION 0° to 65°
TRAVERSE 40°

# 38 cm Raketen Sprenggranate 4581

Largest of all the German field rockets to see service was the 38 cm Raketen Sprenggranate 4581. Originally designed for use in a naval anti-submarine projector the 38 cm rocket was intended for land use as a super-heavy demolition weapon for use in street fighting, the need for which was painfully discovered in the Leningrad and Stalingrad battles. Despite its size the 38 cm was conventional in construction and used a twelve propellant stick motor venting through thirty-two base venturii. The warhead contained 270 lb (122.6 kg) of amatol 50/50 which could have a devastating effect at the short ranges the rocket was intended for. At +15° C the rocket had a maximum range of 6180 yards (5560 m). The rocket had a point-impact nose fuse, some of which were marked with a red ring—this meant the rocket could be transported loaded in its projector, the Raketenwerfer 61. There was one other type of 38 cm rocket, namely the 38 cm Hohladungsgranate 4592 but this differed only in using a hollow charge warhead intended for use against concrete.

# 38 cm Raketenwerfer 61

One of the most unusual of the many novel German rocket projectors was the 38 cm Raketenwerfer 61, built by Rheinmetall-Borsig at their Dusseldorf works. It was unusual on many counts, not the least of which was that it was a projector that routed the rocket's exhaust gases forward on firing. This was even more unusual when it is realised that the projector was breech-loaded. The projector was mounted on a converted Tiger tank with a heavily armoured housing on top to produce the Sturmtiger which was specially developed for street fighting but was built only in small numbers (ten) and too late in the war to have any affect on its progress. The Raketenwerfer when mounted on the Sturmtiger resembled a short, heavy gun, but round the muzzle was a ring of thirty-one holes through which the exhaust gases were vented. As the rocket fired the gases went rearwards but were guided through a two-piece steel obturator ring which also sealed the breech. As the gases left this ring they were forced forward into the space between the barrel and the jacket and out through the muzzle vents. The barrel was rifled to take splines on the rocket base and imparted one turn every 17.6 calibres. Rockets were inserted through a sliding breech and fired via a percussion mechanism. The Sturmtiger carried twelve rockets on internal racks with the option of a further rocket carried in the projector. The crew was five or six men and the vehicle weighed a hefty 70 tons.

**Data** (RW61)

| | | | |
|---|---|---|---|
| OVERALL LENGTH | 2060 mm 81.12 in | ELEVATION | 0° to 85° |
| CALIBRE | 380 mm 14.96 in | TRAVERSE | 20° |
| LENGTH OF LINER (L/4.95) | 1880 mm 74.12 in | | |

**Data**

LENGTH OVERALL (minus fuze)  1439.7 mm
  56.68 in
BODY DIAMETER  380 mm  14.94 in
WEIGHT  345.5 kg ($\pm$5.5 kg)
  761 lb ($\pm$12 lb)
WEIGHT OF PROPELLANT  40.2 kg  88.5 lb
WEIGHT OF EXPLOSIVE  122.6 kg  270 lb
MAXIMUM RANGE (0° C)  5150 m
  5634 yards
MAXIMUM RANGE (15° C)  5560 m
  6180 yards

**Launcher**
38 cm Raketenwerfer 61

*38 cm Raketen Sprenggrantate 4581*

*38 cm Raketenwerfer 61 on Sturmtiger*

# JAPAN

## Japanese Army 20 cm Rocket

In Japan both the Army and the Navy carried out rocket development on similar lines with no centralised control and both produced 20 cm rockets of different designs. The Army rocket was the smaller of the two and was a complete round, unlike the Navy round which was in two halves. In appearance the Army rocket resembled a large artillery shell and had a warhead containing 35.7 lb (16.2 kg) of TNT. The motor vented through six base venturii which imparted the spin stabilisation. Maximum range of this rocket has not been discovered but some reports mention a range of over 3000 yards (2745 m).

## Type 4 Rocket Launcher

At first sight it would be easy to mistake the Type 4 Launcher for a conventional mortar for it used a normal mortar bipod but the barrel had no breech and was open at the base. The launcher fired the 20 cm Army rocket which was loaded by raising part of the top of the barrel. One oddity about this weapon was that it was regarded by the Japanese as a form of heavy mortar and was used more as a means of delivering a heavy projectile accurately than of laying down a heavy area bombardment which is the usual tactical role of the rocket. Normal crew for the Type 4 Launcher was ten men of whom four were ammunition numbers.

**Data**
OVERALL LENGTH 984 mm 38.75 in
DIAMETER 202 mm 7.95 in
WEIGHT 90.8-92.6 kg 200-204 lb
WEIGHT OF MOTOR COMPLETE 42-44.95 kg 92.5-99 lb
WEIGHT OF FILLING 16.2 kg 35.7 lb

**Launcher**
Type 4 Rocket Launcher

**Data**
LENGTH OF TUBE (approx) 1830 mm 72 in
WEIGHT (approx) 227 kg 500 lb

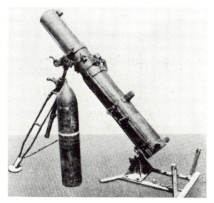

*Type 4 Rocket Launcher*

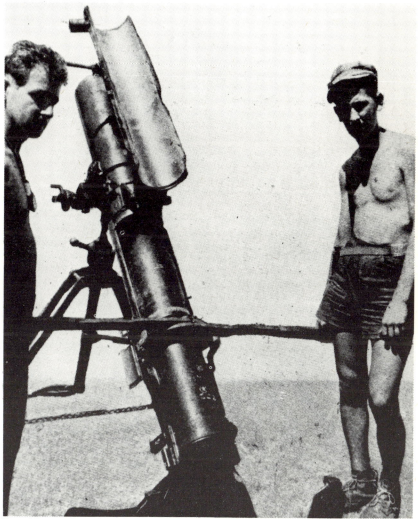

*Type 4 Rocket Launcher with rocket in breech*

# Japanese Navy 20 cm Rocket

More widely encountered than the Army 20 cm rocket was the Navy 20 cm version. This was more of an improvisation than the Army round since it used a standard naval 8 inch shell screwed onto a motor assembly. The motor had seven propellant sticks venting through six base venturii, while the warhead contained 38.6 lb (17.52 kg) of trinitroanisol (TNA). The Navy rocket was often fired from simple wooden rails which were either simply laid along the ground or roughly elevated on wooden legs. These improvised launchers were encountered in combinations of one, two or three sets of rails side-by-side.

## 20 cm Launching Trough

More sophisticated than the crude wooden rails used to launch the Navy 20 cm rocket was the metal trough launcher first encountered on Peleliu in late 1944. This consisted of a trough some 7 to 8 feet long and supported on tubular legs. At the rear two metal brackets held the trough clear of the ground. Elevation and traverse were difficult to set and even more difficult to alter quickly, so the launcher was often used to cover beaches and likely approaches. The elevation was set using a plumb line. Firing was by percussion using a lanyard.

**Data**

| | |
|---|---|
| LENGTH OF TROUGH 2133-2438 mm 84-96 in | HEIGHT OF REAR FROM GROUND 305 mm 12 in |

*20 cm Launching Trough*

## 20 cm Barrel Rocket Projector

The most advanced of the projectors designed for use with the 20 cm Navy rocket was the undesignated device known in Allied intelligence reports as the 20 cm Rocket Projector (Barrel Type). It consisted of a single barrel mounted on a two-wheeled carriage with a short split trail. The overall design was very simple. In action, the wheels were chocked in place (there were no brakes) and an iron mat placed under the breech end to minimise the amount of soil debris thrown up by the exhaust. The barrel was elevated to 5° and the rocket could then be loaded when it was held in place by a sprung cam. After elevating the barrel to the correct angle the rocket could be discharged by a percussion mechanism fired by a lanyard. After firing two or three rounds the barrel became so hot it could not be used for 50-55 minutes. There was a special version produced in very small numbers that was specially designed for pack transport. This had a 84 inch (2133 mm) barrel and weighed about 500 lb (227 kg). The barrel could be broken into two parts and the entire projector could be carried on five pack horses. It used a bipod or tripod mount.

**Data**

| | |
|---|---|
| BARREL LENGTH 1981 mm 78 in | WHEEL DIAMETER 686 mm 27 in |
| DIAMETER 210 mm 8.27 in | WHEEL TRACK 838 mm 33 in |
| TOTAL WEIGHT 236 kg 520 lb | ELEVATION 5° to 75° |

**Data**

| | | |
|---|---|---|
| OVERALL LENGTH | 1041 mm | 41 in |
| DIAMETER | 210 mm | 8.27 in |
| WEIGHT | 90.12 kg | 198.5 lb |
| WEIGHT OF PROPELLANT | 8.3 kg | 18.3 lb |
| WEIGHT OF EXPLOSIVE | 17.52 kg | 38.6 lb |
| MAXIMUM RANGE | 1800 m | 1970 yards |

**Launchers**
20 cm Launching Trough
20 cm Barrel Rocket Projector
20 cm Pack Barrel Projector

*20 cm Launching Trough*

*20 cm Barrel Rocket Projector*

# Type 10 Rocket Motor

**Data**

LENGTH OVERALL (motor)  838 mm  33 in
DIAMETER OF PROPELLANT TUBE  189 mm
 7.44 in
WIDTH OF TAIL  302 mm  11.875 in
WEIGHT OF PROPELLANT  5.875 kg  12.94 lb
BOMB LENGTH  554 mm  21.8 in
BOMB DIAMETER  199.4 mm  7.85 in
WEIGHT OF BOMB  60 kg  132.3 lb
WEIGHT OF HE FILLING  23.2 kg  51 lb

**Launcher**
Type 10 Trough Launcher

One of the very first Japanese rockets to see service was the Type 10 Rocket Motor. The motor resembled a mortar bomb and had three propellant sticks venting through a single venturi in the tail. Four tail fins provided a measure of stabilisation in flight. The motor was used to propel an aerial bomb along a trough launcher. This bomb was the Air Service Bomb Type 97 No. 6. Maximum range achieved by this combination was 1300 yards (1190 m) but accuracy was poor. There were many variations to the basic theme, especially to the motor for it would appear that they were made to a centrally issued design by local units. Firing was effected electrically using a standard commercial blasting contactor.

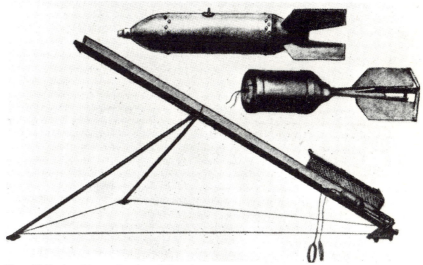

*Type 10 Rocket Motor, Bomb and Trough*

# Enlarged Type 10 Rocket Motor

**Data**

LENGTH OVERALL (motor)  1032 mm
 40.625 in
WEIGHT OF MOTOR  41.7 kg  91.9 lb
WEIGHT OF PROPELLANT  11.35 kg  25 lb
BOMB LENGTH  554 mm  21.8 in
BOMB DIAMETER  199.4 mm  7.85 in
WEIGHT OF BOMB  60 kg  132.3 lb
WEIGHT OF HE FILLING  23.2 kg  51 lb

**Launcher**
Type 10 Trough Launcher

There were many local variations on the basic Type 10 Rocket Motor but one of the more extreme was an undesignated but enlarged version. It used the same construction but was seven inches longer and contained twice as much propellant, again in three sticks. The bigger motor increased the range of the unattached bomb to about 2000 yards (1830 m) but accuracy remained poor. As with the normal Type 10 motor, the bomb was the Type 97 No 6.

*Enlarged Type 19 Rocket Motor and bomb on Type 10 Launcher*

## 250 kg Rocket Bomb

One unusual projectile encountered by Allied troops in 1944 and 1945 was an improvised rocket constructed by removing the tail fins from a standard 250 kg aerial bomb and bolting on a large rocket motor. Not many details of this combination have survived but it is known that it had a range of at least 7500 yards (6863 m) and some reports mention 10000 yards (9150 m). The launcher was a simple trough 273 inches long (6934 mm) and some Allied intelligence reports mention a Lorry-mounted launcher but no details of this have been found.

*250 kg Rocket Bomb*

### Data

| | |
|---|---|
| LENGTH OVERALL (bomb & mortar) 2997 mm 118 in | WEIGHT OF COMBINATION 408.6-431.3 kg 900-950 lb |
| LENGTH OF MOTOR 1981 mm 78 in | WEIGHT OF WARHEAD 250 kg 551.25 lb |
| DIAMETER OF MOTOR 305 mm 12 in | WEIGHT OF HE FILLING 96.25 kg 212 lb |

## Type 10 Trough Launcher

The Type 10 Trough Launcher was first encountered on Peleliu Island in late 1944 and was used in conjunction with the Type 10 Rocket Motor and Type 96 Bomb. It was a simple wood and metal trough supported on two iron tube legs which could be placed at different angles by a simple cord-and-ring arrangement tied to the baseplate. In action, the launcher was usually emplaced in a pit. The rocket motor was placed on the rail and over the blunt nose of the motor was placed a wooden ring. Onto this ring was placed the bomb and its fins were wedged into the ring. After the electrical connections had been made the rocket would be fired from a distance. These launchers were used also on Saipan and Iwo Jima.

### Data

| | |
|---|---|
| LENGTH OVERALL | 6045 mm 238 in |
| LENGTH OF LEGS | 3759 mm 148 in |
| WIDTH OF TROUGH AT BASE | 216 mm 8.5 in |
| WIDTH OF TROUGH AT TOP | 152 mm 6 in |
| HEIGHT AT 30° | 3353 mm 132 in |
| ELEVATION | 30° to 50° in 5° steps |

## 44.7 cm Rocket

The largest rocket used in action by the Japanese was an undesignated 44.7 cm projectile, often referred to in Allied reports as the 45 cm rocket. It was used in action on Luzon and Iwo Jima and like so many Japanese rockets was a crude and roughly-made improvisation bought about to compensate for their lack of heavy artillery. It used spin stabilisation through six base venturii through which flowed the exhaust gases from the forty sticks of propellant used in the motor. The warhead contained 398 lb (180.7 kg) of Type 98 explosive which was sometimes replaced by picric acid. A crude wooden trough launcher was used with this rocket but each launcher was used only once since the rocket usually demolished the wooden framework. Maximum range was 2140 yards (1958 m).

### Data

| | |
|---|---|
| LENGTH OVERALL | 1714.5 mm 67.5 in |
| BODY DIAMETER | 447 mm 17.6 in |
| WEIGHT | 682.8 kg 1504 lb |
| WEIGHT OF PROPELLANT | 59.25 kg 130.5 lb |
| WEIGHT OF EXPLOSIVE | 180.7 kg 398 lb |

*44.7 cm Rockets on their wooden launchers*

# UNITED KINGDOM

## 2-inch Rocket

**Data**
LENGTH OVERALL   914.4 mm   36 in
BODY DIAMETER   57 mm   2.25 in
WEIGHT   4.88 kg   10.75 lb
MAXIMUM VELOCITY   457 m/s   1500 ft/sec
WEIGHT OF HE FILLING   0.25 kg   0.56 lb

The 2-inch rocket was the first of the British rockets to be developed but was soon overtaken by development work carried out on the heavier 3-inch rocket. Work on the 2-inch rocket was continued but it was not developed to any great extent and was used mainly for secondary tasks such as defence of merchant ships and target illumination. The basic 2-inch rocket was a simple conventional device using a single stick of SCRK (solventless cordite) propellant which was electrically ignited. A nose-mounted No. 720 fuze was a direct-action wind vane armed device with a built-in self destruct timer which operated after 4.5 seconds at a height of about 4500 feet (1372.5 m). The motor burned for 1.2 seconds and was launched after burning for 0.1 seconds. Without the self destruct mechanism the rocket could reach 10000 feet (3050 m).

## 2-inch Rocket Mounting, Mk. II, Pillar Box

There were several types of naval launcher for the 2-inch rocket but only one was used on land. This was the Mark II, or Pillar Box mount which was used on coastal sites along the South Coast of the UK for local AA defence. It derived its name from the shape of a central cabinet which housed the operator and his controls. Arranged on the two sides of the mounting were twenty rockets, ten on each side. They could be fired in two salvoes of ten or all together. The firing circuits were electrical and the firing circuits were made by pressing foot pedals. Traverse was 360° and elevation from 0° to +85° Only HE rockets were fired.

*Practice loading of a land-based Pillar Box mounting*

# 3-inch Rocket (U.P.)

Work on the British rockets began in 1934 and was carried out by a team led by Dr. Crow, a Woolwich Arsenal physicist. The first result was the 2-inch rocket but in 1937 the Sub-Committee on Air Defence Research requested that priority be given to a 3-inch rocket which would have the same warhead weight as the 3.7 inch AA gun shell. The intention was to use the rockets to supplement the guns. The new projectile was known as the 3″U.P. (unrotated projectile) and trial firings were carried out at a range at Aberporth in South Wales but much of the trial design work was carried out at Fort Halstead in Kent. In 1939 extensive firing trials were carried out in Jamaica and the 3-inch rocket was then passed for service use. The first operational 'Z' battery using the 3-inch rocket was set up near Cardiff, but the first German aircraft to be brought down by a rocket was claimed by the Aberporth trial battery. The first 3-inch rocket, the Mark 1, was a conventional design using a single tube of SCRK cordite and was fin-stabilised. A special time fuze, the No. 700 Mark 1 was fitted to the first rockets but this was developed into more advanced electro-magnetic forms.

**Data** (Mark 1)

LENGTH OVERALL  1930 mm  76 in
BODY DIAMETER  82.6 mm  3.25 in
WEIGHT  24.5 kg  53.97 lb
WEIGHT OF PROPELLANT  5.76 kg  12.7 lb
WEIGHT OF HE FILLING  1.94 kg  4.28 lb
MAXIMUM VELOCITY  457 m/s  1500 ft/sec
LAUNCHING VELOCITY  61 m/s  200 ft/sec
MAXIMUM CEILING (unlimited)  6770 m  22200 ft
HORIZONTAL RANGE (unlimited)  3720 m  12200 ft

**Launchers**
Projector, 3-inch, Mark 1
Projector, Rocket, 3-inch, No. 2 Mark 1
Projector, Rocket, 3-inch, No. 4 Marks 1 and 2
Projector, Rocket, 3-inch, No. 6 Mark 1

*Loading a 3-inch Rocket into a **Mark 1** Launcher*

## Projector, 3-inch, Mark 1

The first of the British 3-inch projectors was made by Messrs. G. A. Harvey of Greenwich who produced a batch of ten within six weeks of being issued with the first design drawings and by September 1940 had produced one thousand projectors out of a total requirement of 2500. Involved in the design were both BSA and Vickers-Armstrong, but the design was known to the Army as the Mark 1 and to the Navy as the 3-inch Harvey L.S. Projector (the Navy actually used very few of them and most of their allocation went to the Merchant Navy). The Mark 1 was a very simple device firing a single rocket from two guide rails. There were no fire controls on the launcher—the layer on the right behind a shield pushed the rails into the general direction of the target using very simple sights and the rails were then locked in place by another member of the team on the left of the rails. The rocket was then fired electrically. The first trial battery was formed in October 1940 at Aberporth and later batteries were manned by Home Guard units. Many Mark 1 projectors were used for training and trials.

**Data**

| | | |
|---|---|---|
| LENGTH OF RAILS  3658 mm  144 in | WIDTH  2372 mm  93.375 in |
| WEIGHT (approx)  50 kg  112 lb | LENGTH  3658 mm  144 in |
| HEIGHT DEPRESSED  2235 mm  88 in | ELEVATION  0° to 70° |
| | TRAVERSE  360° |

2

*1, 2. Projector, 3-inch Mark 1 or No 1*

*A Z battery in action at a demonstration*

# Projector, Rocket, 3-inch, No. 2 Mark 1

The first British projector to be used on a large scale was the No. 2 Mark 1 which could fire one or two 3-inch rockets. Four guide rails were used, two to a rocket. Elevation was by handwheel and traversing by a crank and the firing current came from a battery. Laying was by two men, one traversing on the left, one elevating on the right. The mounting was either emplaced in concrete or was secured to a No. 2 firing platform. One battery equipped with the No. 2 projector served in North Africa and was used to defend ports, including Tobruk.

**Data**

| | | | | | |
|---|---|---|---|---|---|
| LENGTH OF RAILS | 3658 mm | 144 in | WIDTH | 2721 mm | 107.125 in |
| WEIGHT | 566.14 kg | 1247 lb | LENGTH | 3734 mm | 147 in |
| HEIGHT (full elevation) | 3937 mm | 155 in | ELEVATION | 10° to 80° | |
| | | | TRAVERSE | 360° | |

*Home Guards loading a No 2 Mark 1 Projector*

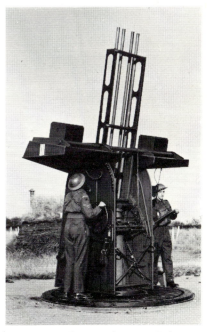

*Projector, Rocket, 3-inch, No 2 Mark 1*

# Projector, Rocket, 3-inch, No. 4 Marks 1 and 2

A more complex and mobile launcher for the 3-inch rocket was provided by the No. 4 equipment. This consisted of a nine-rocket projector consisting of thirty-six rails arranged so that each rocket was supported by two long and two short rails when fired. The rails were arranged in vertical banks. There were two basic variants, the Mark 1 and Mark 2, but the Mark 2 differed only in being equipped with an electro-magnetic fuze-setting device. The two layers were situated in two small metal cabins, one on each side of the rails, and controlled the projector in traverse and elevation. The travelling platform for the projector was derived from that of the 3-inch AA mounting platform. There were four main types of platform. The No. 2 Mark 1 was originally the Mark 3A 3-inch AA mounting platform, the No. 2 Mark 1A was the Mark 3B, the Mark 1B was the Mark 1VA, and the Mark 1C originated as the Mark 1VB. The projectors could be mounted on any one of these platforms. All nine rockets could be fired in ¾ second in four salvoes of 3, 2, 2, 2. One hundred of these equipments were produced to form eight batteries, and two of these batteries were used in North Africa.

## Data

LENGTH OF LONG GUIDE RAILS  3658 mm  144 in
LENGTH OF SHORT GUIDE RAILS  2184 mm  84 in
TOTAL WEIGHT  7500 kg  16520 lb
LENGTH OVERALL  7125 mm  280.5 in
HEIGHT TRAVELLING  3886 mm  153 in
HEIGHT FULLY ELEVATED  5486 mm  216 in
WIDTH  2464 mm  97 in
ELEVATION  7° to 75°
TRAVERSE  360°

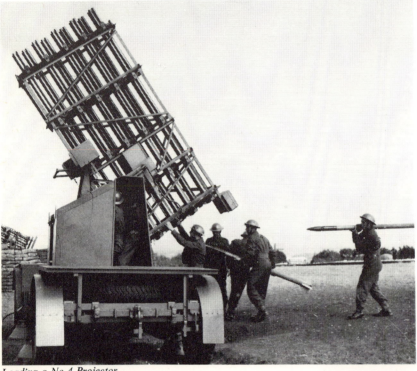

*Loading a No 4 Projector*

*Projector, Rocket, 3-inch, No 4 Mark 2*

*No 4 Projector in action*

# Projector, Rocket, 3-inch, No. 6 Mark 1

**Data**
LENGTH OF GUIDE RAILS   3632 mm   143 in
WEIGHT COMPLETE   7118 kg   15680 lb
  (7 tons)
LENGTH AT 20°   4724 mm   186 in
LENGTH AT 80°   2515 mm   99 in
HEIGHT AT 20°   3962 mm   156 in
HEIGHT AT 80°   4800 mm   189 in
WIDTH OVERALL   3200 mm   126 in
WIDTH OF CABIN   838 mm   33 in
ELEVATION   20° to 80°
TRAVERSE   345°

Largest of all the British rocket projectors was the No. 6. It was a fixed projector using twenty sets of guide rails to fire twenty rockets. They were arranged in two sets of ten on each side of a central control cabin housing the two gun layers. All the rails were controlled together and all the rockets were fired in ¾ second in four salvoes of 6,4,6,4. The firing circuit was electrically supplied by a 7.2 volt battery and the circuit was made by a foot switch. At the front of the control cabin the elevation layer sat behind a window with simple sights provided. The traverse layer stood behind him with another set of sights and a window in the roof. Both were in contact with a central command post. The No. 6 entered service in 1944.

*Projector, Rocket, 3-inch, No 6 Mark 1*

*No 6 Projector from the rear*

*No 6 Projectors in use—note the spread of the rockets*

## Land Mattress Rocket

**Data** (Motor, Rocket, Aircraft, 3-inch,
  No. 1 Marks 2 and 3)
LENGTH COMPLETE   1770 mm   69.7 in
LENGTH OF MOTOR   1402 mm   55.2 in
WEIGHT COMPLETE   30.53 kg   67.25 lb
WEIGHT OF PROPELLANT   5 kg   11 lb
WEIGHT OF HE FILLING   3.18 kg   7 lb
MAXIMUM VELOCITY   335 m/s   1100 ft/sec
MAXIMUM RANGE   7230 m   7900 yards

The first attempts to produce a British artillery rocket system were not very successful mainly due to the rocket dispersion and low range. Early attempts involved a 5-inch rocket which was rejected by the Army. The Navy took up the idea after it had been rejected and installed the Army equipment in the LCT(R). Each LVT(R) carried 1080 5-inch rockets which were fired from the Army six-barrel projectors arranged in banks. The 5-inch rocket had a range of 3800 yards (3477 m) which was adequate for bombarding beaches but not for more prolonged use on land. Further development of basic rocket principles showed that accuracy and range could be improved if a finned rocket was rotated slightly when launched and this was applied to an aircraft 3-inch No. 1 motor to which the naval 29 lb shell was fitted. Range was increased to 8000 yards (7320 m) but the launcher that was developed for this combination, the 'Land Mattress' (the original naval 5-inch equipment was the 'Mattress') could be elevated only between 23° and 45°. This limited the minimum range to 6700 yards (6130 m) so lower ranges were accommodated by placing a rotary spoiler over the rocket exhaust which could be partially closed to limit the escaping gases and thus limit the range. There were three different spoilers available which gave a combination of ranges down to 3900 yards (3568 m). The motor used a single cordite stick which was cruciform in cross-section, and which burned for 1.6 seconds. A special 3-inch warhead was designed for use with this rocket but it does not appear to have seen service.

*Land Mattress Rocket*

# Land Mattress

The first launcher developed to fire the 3-inch artillery rocket was a 32-barrel projector built onto a standard 20 cwt G.S. trailer. It was produced by the Ministry of Supply in May 1944 and another experimental version was built with forty barrels. The Canadian First Army asked for a twelve-launcher battery after a demonstration in July 1944 and these went into action on 1st November 1944 during the crossing of the Scheldt. The projectors, named Land Mattress, were a great success and fired 1146 rounds during a six-hour period.

As a result of the success of the Land Mattress the design was formalised into the Projector, Rocket, 3-inch, No. 8 Mark 1. The basic design was the same as the earlier projector and differed only in detail construction methods. Thirty barrels were arranged in five horizontal rows of six, each loaded from the front. Rockets were fired at $\frac{1}{4}$ second intervals so that the entire salvo could be fired in $7\frac{1}{4}$ seconds. The projectors were laid as conventional artillery pieces using Dial Sight No. 9 and a Sight Clinometer Mark IV. By the time the No. 8 had been produced in quantity (by Tillings Stevens Ltd) the war in Europe was almost over and some were sent to South-East Asia, but it is not known if any saw action. To give an idea of the dispersion of the rockets used in the No. 8 the 50% zone of a salvo at 6000 yards (5490 m) was 235 yards long by 240 yards wide (215 × 219 m).

It was appreciated that the No. 8 projector would be too heavy for jungle warfare so a lightened version using sixteen barrels was developed to be towed by a Jeep. It did not see service before the war ended. Weight was 835 lb (379 kg).

**Data** (Projector, Rocket, 3-inch, No. 8 Mark 1)
LENGTH OF BARRELS   1480 mm   58.25 in
PITCH OF RAILS   One turn in 100 in (2540 mm)
WEIGHT UNLOADED   1118.6 kg   2464 lb
WEIGHT LOADED   2034.6 kg   4481.5 lb
LENGTH OVERALL   3226 mm   127 in
HEIGHT TRAVELLING   1765 mm   69.5 in
WHEEL TRACK   1702 mm   67 in
ELEVATION   23° to 45°
TRAVERSE   20°
ROTATION OF PROJECTILE   660 rotations per minute

*Land Mattress*

*Projector, Rocket, 3-inch, No 8 Mark 1*

*Loading a Land Mattress No 8 Mark 1*

# LILO Rockets

By 1944 the use by the Japanese of heavily fortified bunkers and strong-points was becoming an established feature of warfare in the Pacific and South-East Asia. As a possible counter to these difficult-to-counter positions the rocket was suggested and special single-round projectors were developed. The American version emerged as the M12 but the British projector had a more protracted development before the Projector, Rocket, 3-inch, No. 10 Mark 1 was passed for service use. The code name of LILO was given to the projector which could fire two types of rocket. Both rockets used the same motor, the Motor, rocket, 3-inch, No. 7 Mark 1 but the heads varied in weight. One used the Shell, HE 21 lb, No. 5 rocket, 3-inch Mark 1, and the other the Shell, HE 60 lb, No. 6 rocket, 3-inch Mark 1. Both were intended for use at very short ranges but were rotated in the launcher barrel to prevent too much dispersion. Firing was electrical using a 3.4 volt battery.

## Data

| | |
|---|---|
| Motor, Rocket, 3-inch, No. 7 Mark 1 | WEIGHT  9.53 kg  21 lb |
| LENGTH OVERALL (motor)  876 mm  34.5 in | WEIGHT OF HE FILLING  1.8 kg  4 lb |
| LENGTH WITH 21 LB SHELL  1238 mm 48.75 in | Shell, HE 60 lb, No. 6 Rocket, 3-inch, Mark 1 |
| LENGTH WITH 60 LB SHELL  1321 mm 52 in | LENGTH  444.5 mm  17.5 in |
| BODY DIAMETER  82.55 mm  3.25 in | DIAMETER  152 mm  6 in |
| WEIGHT (motor only)  8.3 kg  18.25 lb | WEIGHT  27.25 kg  60 lb |
| WEIGHT OF PROPELLANT  1.93 kg  4.25 lb | WEIGHT OF HE FILLING  6.24 kg  13.75 lb |
| | Complete round |
| Shell, HE 21 lb, No. 5 Rocket, 3-inch, Mark 1 | WEIGHT WITH 21 LB SHELL  17.82 kg 39.25 lb |
| LENGTH  362 mm  14.25 in | WEIGHT WITH 60 LB SHELL  35.5 kg 78.25 lb |
| DIAMETER  82.55 mm  3.25 in | |

# Projector, Rocket, 3-inch, No. 10 Mark 1 (LILO)

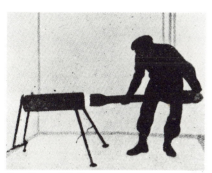

*Loading a LILO*

LILO was a simple one-round rocket launcher intended for use at close ranges against strongly fortified bunkers in South-East Asia. The projector was designed to be carried by one man with another carrying the rocket and was laid by using open sights at close ranges. The folding front legs were of a fixed length but the tube could be raised and lowered on the U-shaped back leg for changes in elevation. The rockets used with the LILO were both capable of penetrating 10 feet of earth and at least one layer of logs. The accuracy of the equipment was such that five rounds had to be fired at a target 50 yards away to be sure of a 95% chance of hitting the target.

### Data

| | |
|---|---|
| LENGTH OF BARREL  711 mm  28 in | LENGTH OF FRONT LEGS  635 mm  25 in |
| DEPTH OF RAILS  56 mm  2.2 in | WEIGHT  16.8 kg  37 lb |
| PITCH OF RAILS (R.H.)  One turn in 48 in (1219 mm) | |

# Tulip

In 1944 a unit of the Coldstream Guards with the Guards Armoured Division 'borrowed' some aircraft rockets from a nearby Typhoon squadron and fitted them on launcher rails, one on each side of their Sherman V and VC tank turrets. The rocket added considerably to the striking power of the unit, but the arrangement, code-named Tulip, was not adopted for general use. The rocket used utilised the Motor, rocket, aircraft, 3-inch, No. 1 but the exact Mark is uncertain, as is the type of launching rail used. The rocket used a Shell, HE, 60 lb S.A.P., No. 1 or 2, but again the exact Mark is uncertain. The HE filling weighed about 14 lb (6.35 kg).

*Tulip aboard a Sherman*

# USA

## Rocket, H.E.A.T., 2.36-Inch, M6A1 and M6A3

Final development of the 2.36 inch rocket that was to become one of the most potent anti-tank weapons of World War 2 began in early 1942. Some research work into rockets had begun in 1933 at Aberdeen Proving Grounds but it was not until 1942 that work began in earnest. The first 2.36 inch rockets were used in action in November 1942 and thereafter were used in all theatres of the War. There were two main 2.36 inch rockets—the M6A1 and M6A3. Of these the M6A1 was the most widely used. Both types used hollow charge heads, but the M6A1 had a pointed nose and swept fins while the M6A3 had a rounded nose and drum fins. They both used the same rocket motor and both could be fired from M1, M9 and M18 Rocket Launchers, more popularly known as 'bazookas'. In action the rockets were carried by one man of a two-man team who usually carried two canvas bags each containing three rockets. Maximum effective range against armour was 300 yards (275 m). On occasion the rockets could be buried to form anti-tank mines and were sometimes placed and fired close to structures for demolition work. Captured examples of 2.36 inch rockets were used by the Germans as the basis for their 8.8 cm rocket series.

**Data**
LENGTH OVERALL (M6A1)   549 mm   21.6 in
LENGTH OVERALL (M6A3)   493 mm   19.4 in
BODY DIAMETER   60 mm   2.36 in
WEIGHT   1.54 kg   3.4 lb
WEIGHT OF PROPELLANT   0.056 kg   0.12 lb
WEIGHT OF WARHEAD   0.227 kg   0.5 lb
VELOCITY (70° F)   82 m/s   270 ft/sec
MAXIMUM RANGE   640 m   700 yards

**Launchers**
Launcher M1, M1A1, M9, M18

*Loading a Bazooka*

*Rocket, HEAT, 2.36-inch, M6A1*

## Rocket, H.E., 4.5-Inch, M8

The 4.5-inch rocket was produced and used in larger numbers than any other rocket in use during World War 2. It was used on land, for bombarding beaches from ships and landing craft, and with very little modification could be used for firing from aircraft. This section is devoted to its use against land targets when fired from land-based launchers but even so the list of launchers is long. The 4.5-inch rocket started life as the T22 but was developed into the M8 series. It used folding tail fins for stabilisation and a nose-fused warhead. Construction was conventional and the motor used ballistite sticks (thirty) venting through a single venturi. Firing could be either electrical, percussion or by using a black powder igniter depending on the type of launcher in use. Variants were the M8A1 with a strengthened motor body for use in a wide range of climates, the M8A2 with a smaller heavier-walled warhead, and the M8A3 which was the M8A2 with some minor changes to the fins. By August 1945 2,537,000 4.5 inch rockets had been procured.

**Data**

| | |
|---|---|
| LENGTH OVERALL   838 mm   33 in | WEIGHT OF PROPELLANT (M8A3)   2.11 kg   4.65 lb |
| BODY DIAMETER   114 mm   4.5 in | |
| DIAMETER OF OPEN FINS   3.5 mm   12 in | WEIGHT OF HE FILLING   1.95 kg   4.3 lb |
| WEIGHT   17.5 kg   38.5 lb | VELOCITY (70° F)   259 m/s   850 ft/sec |
| WEIGHT OF PROPELLANT (T22)   2.16 kg   4.75 lb | MAXIMUM RANGE   4209 m   4600 yards |

*4.5-inch rockets being fuzed*

# 4.5-Inch Rocket Launchers

A wide range of launchers for use with the 4.5 inch rockets was developed but only a few actually saw operational service. Listed below are the main types.

T27 Multiple Rocket Launcher. This carried eight rockets. It was mounted on the GMC $2\frac{1}{2}$T $6\times6$ and Studebaker $2\frac{1}{2}$T $6\times4$. There was no traversing mechanism but elevation was from $-5°$ to $+45°$. The M6 telescopic sight and T100 mount were used with this equipment.

T27E1 Multiple Rocket Launcher. As the T27 but the launcher could be disassembled for transport.

T27E2 Multiple Rocket Launcher. On this launcher the rocket capacity was increased to twenty-four in three layers of eight tubes.

T28 Multiple Rocket Launcher. This was the T27E2 with square launching frames instead of tubes.

T34 (Calliope). This large capacity (sixty) launcher was fitted above the turret of the M4 Medium Tank. The sixty tubes were approximately 10 feet (3050 mm) long and were made of plywood. Elevation and traverse changes were made by moving the turret controls and the entire launcher could be jettisoned in an emergency. The tubes were arranged in two top banks of eighteen tubes with two six-bank rows underneath. Loading was from the rear and the tubes were discarded after firing two or three salvoes. The T34 was used in Europe from 1944 onwards.

T34E1. This variant of the basic T34 was fitted to the M4A1 Medium Tank and featured a rearrangement of the tubes. The top rows consisted of only sixteen tubes while the bottom rows increased to seven-tube banks. This configuration decreased the dispersion of a salvo.

T34E2. As T34A1, but the tubes were replaced by square launchers.

T44. This launcher was fitted to the DUKW or Landing Vehicle LVT(A4). It carried 120 rockets on a fixed mount with no variation for traverse or elevation.

T45. Fitted to the M24 Light Tank and LVT(A4), the T45 could be fitted in pairs (one to each side) to the $\frac{1}{4}$ ton Truck $4\times4$. Each launcher carried fourteen rockets. They were also fitted to the 1 ton $4\times4$ (International). There were no traverse controls but the launcher could be elevated up to $+35°$.

M12 Rocket Launcher. Originally the T35, the M12 was a single round launcher made of plastic. It consisted of a tube with two front legs and one rear and was used to demolish strong points and such targets as caves. Barrel length was 48 inches (1219 mm) and weight with a rocket loaded was 52 lb (23.6 kg). The launcher was carried on two slings.

M12A1. Externally similar to the basic M12.

M12E1. As M12 but made of magnesium alloy. This launcher could be reused, unlike the basic M12 which was discarded after one launching. The M12E1 also featured an adjustable rear leg.

Scorpion. This was a special DUKW conversion that carried 144 launcher tubes. It saw action in small numbers in New Guinea.

*T27 Multiple Rocket Launchers mounted in units of two on GMC $2\frac{1}{2}$T 6x6 cargo trucks*

*Loading a T27 launcher*

*The combination of hand generator and switch needed to fire a T27*

Loading a Calliope

T34E1

T45 Multiple Rocket Launcher loaded with M8A2 rockets

T44 Multiple Rocket Launcher fitted to a DUKW

T45 Multiple Rocket Launcher mounted on the Truck, 1 ton, 4x4
(International) manned by USMC

## Rocket, H.E., 4.5-Inch, M16

**Data**
LENGTH OVERALL   787 mm   31 in
BODY DIAMETER   114 mm   4.5 in
WEIGHT   19.3 kg   42.5 lb
WEIGHT OF PROPELLANT   2.16 kg   4.75 lb
WEIGHT OF HE FILLING   2.36 kg   5.2 lb
VELOCITY (70° F)   253 m/s   830 ft/sec
MAXIMUM RANGE (45°)   4804 m   5250 yards

**Launcher**
Launcher, Rocket, Multiple 4.5-inch, T66

Despite the success of the 4.5 inch M8 rockets it was decided that accuracy was not good enough for it to become an artillery rocket. As a result of tests carried out with captured German rockets and other research trials it was decided to produce a spin-stabilised 4.5 inch rocket and this, in time, became the M16. Its construction was conventional enough for a 'spinner', and it entered service in Europe just as the war was ending. Reports on its accuracy were good and range was increased over the M8. Later development included a version for use on aircraft.

## Launcher, Rocket, Multiple 4.5-Inch, T66

The twenty-four barrelled launcher known as the T66 was designed to fire the spin-stabilised M16 rocket. Its career during World War 2 was very short as it arrived in Germany in early May 1945 and took part in only one engagement before the war ended. They were issued to 282nd Field Artillery Battalion, 8th Corps, 1st Army. The T66 was muzzle loaded and the rockets were kept in the barrels by fixed back-stops. It took about ninety seconds to load the launcher and the rockets could then be fired in a ripple lasting two seconds.

*A T66 in action in Germany, 1945*

**Data**

| | | | | | |
|---|---|---|---|---|---|
| LENGTH OF BARRELS | 914 mm | 36 in | WEIGHT UNLOADED | 544.8 kg | 1200 lb |
| LENGTH OVERALL | 3048 mm | 120 in | WEIGHT LOADED | 1007.9 kg | 2220 lb |
| HEIGHT AT 0° ELEVATION | 1092 mm | 43 in | ELEVATION | 0° to 45° | |
| | | | TRAVERSE | 20° | |

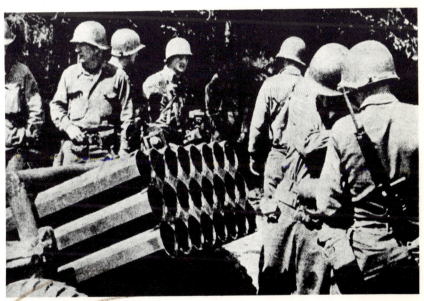

*Loading a T66*

## 7.2-Inch Rockets

**Data (T37/M25)**
LENGTH OVERALL   889/1270 mm   35/50 in
WARHEAD DIAMETER   183 mm   7.2 in
WEIGHT   27.7/23.5 kg   61/51.8 lb
WEIGHT OF FILLING (HE/chem)   13.6/9.1 kg   30/20 lb
VELOCITY (max)   48.8/207 m/s   160/680 ft/sec
RANGE   210/3138 m   230/3430 yards

**Launchers**
M17(T40) 'Whiz-bang'

The Army 7.2 inch rocket had its origins in a British Navy rocket, the Hedgehog, which was intended for use against submarines in place of the more conventional depth charge. When the need for a short-range demolition rocket became apparent the American copy of the British Hedgehog (the ASR) was redesignated T37, but was often referred to as the DR (demolition rocket). It had a high payload to weight ratio and it used a 2.25 inch rocket motor with drum fins.

Range of the T37 was only 230 yards (210 m) and a range increase was desirable so a quick improvisation was brought about by fitting the 4.5 inch T22 rocket motor. The result became the T57 with a range of 1200 yards (1098 m). One further variant was the T21 Chemical rocket which was standardised as the M25. It used a smaller warhead with a variety of possible fillings, but the only one used in action was smoke. Due to its smaller warhead the rocket had a range of 3430 yards (3138 m).

# Launcher, Rocket, Multiple 7.2-Inch, M17

There were many different types of launcher developed for the 7.2 inch rocket but only one type, the M17, actually saw any service. The M17 was a twenty-rocket box launcher mounted over the turret of an M4 medium tank and was also fitted to the M4A1, M4A2, M4A3, M4A4 and M4A6. The front of the launcher was connected with the tank gun barrel and could thus be elevated by using the normal gun mechanisms. In an emergency the launcher could be jettisoned, but normally the rockets were fired singly or in salvoes. Loading was from the front. The M17 saw action in Europe from 1944 onwards and soon earned itself the nickname 'Whiz-bang'. Original designation for the M17 was T40.

**Data**

| | | |
|---|---|---|
| LENGTH OF LAUNCHER | 2667 mm | 105 in |
| WIDTH OF LAUNCHER | 2667 mm | 105 in |
| WEIGHT EMPTY | 2095 kg | 4615 lb |
| ELEVATION | −5° to +25° | |
| TRAVERSE | 360° | |

*Loading a M17 Launcher with 7.2-inch rockets*

# American Rocket Propulsion Units

In order to give the infantry a short range support weapon that could be used to demolish strong-points the basic 4.5-inch T22(M8) motor was fitted to a 100 lb G.P. bomb to produce the Rocket, H.E., 8-inch, T25. This device was used in small numbers in the Pacific Theatre. It was transported and fired from the 8-inch Rocket Launcher T53 which was a square steel framework supported at the front by two tube legs.

A heavier payload was possible by combining three basic T22 rocket motors to form the Propulsion Unit, Jet, T13. The exhausts of this unit were combined to vent through a single manifold and the warhead was either a 250 or 500 lb G.P. bomb. Both H.E. and napalm fillings were used. The T13 was launched from a converted 105 mm howitzer carriage in which the barrel was replaced by a V-shaped trough. This was the T103 launcher which used the Panoramic Telescope, M1, normally fitted to the 75 mm Pack Howitzer M1A1. It saw limited service in the Pacific during the last months of the War.

*T53 8-inch Rocket Launcher*

*T103 Launcher in action on Iwo Jima*

*Rocket, HE, 8-inch, T25*

# USSR

## Preliminary Note on Russian Rockets

Of all the combatant nations that used rocket weapons during World War 2, the most difficult to discover anything about is undoubtedly Russia. The amount of secrecy lavished on their rockets by the Soviets during the war years was such that even today more is known about Russian post-war rockets than is known about their early versions. The section on Russian rocketry is therefore less fully documented and covered than that given to other nations. The reason for the secrecy dates back to the early 1930s when the Gas Dynamic Laboratory at Leningrad started research on rockets for war purposes. Similar work was being carried out in other countries but little of the Russian work was leaked out and few were even aware that the Russians had rockets at all. The result was a 'secret weapon' mentality which was taken as far as using only police or NKVD troops to actually man the rocket launchers. In transit, the launchers were kept completely covered. The first rocket units went into action on 15 July 1941 and were at first called 'Kostikov's Guns' after Andre Kostikov who completed the design work on the launchers started by an Army engineer named Petropavlovsky until his death in 1935. This name was soon dropped in favour of the well-known 'Katyusha' which (although strictly speaking should apply only to the M-8 launcher), was soon applied to the whole range of Russian rockets. In time, rocket units were formed among the regular units of the Russian armies and some propaganda photographs were released but these tell us little about the actual make-up of the rockets and the propellants used. It is safe to assume that the most common propellant was a form of solventless cordite, but some references mention the use of ordinary black powder. All the wartime rockets used fin stabilisation and were fired from open rail launchers. One other item that should be mentioned is that it is not possible to give a full coverage to the full range of vehicles that carried the rocket launcher frames. An enormous variety of vehicles was used for this purpose including Lease-Lend and captured vehicles and even T-60 and T-70 light tanks—a full coverage is just not possible.

## 82 mm Rocket

The first 82 mm rockets were used in action near Orszy in July 1941 and were soon greatly feared by the German troops who had to endure their devastating bombardments. The 82 mm rockets were used mainly in high explosive form but there was a special RS-82 rocket which had a high-fragmentation warhead.

*M-8 launcher on Lease-Lend 6x4 Studebaker 2½-ton truck*

*M-8 82 mm launcher mounted on ZIS-6 2½-ton truck*

**Data**

| | | | | | | |
|---|---|---|---|---|---|---|
| OVERALL LENGTH | 596 mm | 23.5 in | WEIGHT OF WARHEAD | 3.05 kg | 6.725 lb | |
| DIAMETER | 82 mm | 3.23 in | WEIGHT OF PROPELLANT | 1 kg | 2.2 lb | |
| WEIGHT | 8 kg | 17.6 lb | RANGE | 5500 m | 6017 yards | |
| | | | M.V. | 315 m/s | 1033 ft/sec | |

## M-8 Launcher

One of the most widely used of all the Russian launchers was the M-8 which was mounted on a ZIS-6 truck as a standard fitting, but was sometimes fitted to other vehicles. The M-8 carried 36 82 mm rockets in three rows. On top were fourteen rockets, under them was a row of twelve and slung under the bottom row were ten rockets. The launcher rails were perforated steel beams attached to a steel tube frame. The rails were about 74 inches (1880 mm) long and could be elevated from +15° to +45° and traversed 10° using controls on the left of the vehicle. The rockets were fired electrically via primers in the rocket venturii using power from a battery in the cab which was protected by a steel sheet over the roof. Ripple firing was brought about by a rotary switch box, but the minimum number that could be fired was two rockets.

A variant was the M8-48 mounted on the GAZ 63 which appeared in 1944. This carried 48 rockets and was unusual in that the rails faced to the rear when travelling.

A 1941 variant was a special eight-rocket frame introduced for mountain troops.

# 132 mm Rocket

Introduced just after the 82 mm rocket the 132 mm was the result of research started in 1933. In time it became by far the most widely used of all the Russian rockets and served on for many years after the war.

**Data**
LENGTH OVERALL   1420 mm   55.9 in
DIAMETER   132 mm   5.2 in
WEIGHT   42.5 kg   93.7 lb

WEIGHT OF WARHEAD   18.5 kg   40.8 lb
WEIGHT OF PROPELLANT   7.08 kg   15.6 lb
M.V.   355 m/s   1165 ft/sec
RANGE   8500 m   9300 yards

*132 mm rockets on M-13 launcher*

# M-13 Launcher

The M-13 could carry 16 132 mm rockets on eight I-section steel rails arranged eight on top and eight underneath held on studs fixed to the rocket bodies. The rails were 192 inches long (4877 mm) and were supported on a steel tube frame similar to that used on the M-8. Elevation was limited to a maximum of 45°. Traverse was either 10° or 20° according to the chassis used. The sight used was a MP41 dial sight normally used for mortars. The first of many vehicles to carry the M-13 were the ZIS-6 and ZIS-150 trucks which were replaced after 1944 by the GAZ-63. Other vehicles used were the T-60 and T-70 light tank chassis. Variants of the basic M-13 were the M-13-UK which gave an increased dispersion to cover a wider area with fire and the later M-13-DD which was used with an improved rocket to give a range of up to 1100 m(1203 yards).

*M-13 launcher on ZIS-6 truck*

*M-13 on T-60 light tank chassis*  *M-13 on STZ-5 artillery tractor*  *Loading M-13 launchers*

## 300 mm Rocket

The 300 mm rocket was produced in 1942 and was fired from four-rocket static racks. These frames were not unlike the German schweres Wurfgerät 40 or 41 in general appearance and like them they were usually emplaced for 'set-piece' barrages. The rocket weighed 72 kg (158.75 lb) and it had a range of up to 2800 m (3063 yards), and the frames were referred to as the M-30 frame.

*300 mm rockets being launched from M-30 frames*

# 310 mm Rockets

There were two main variants of the 310 mm rockets. The first was produced in 1943 and had a weight of 92.5 kg (204 lb) and a range of up to 4800 m (5250 yards). It was fired from the M-30 frame in the same way as the 300 mm rocket. The second 310 mm rocket appeared in 1944 and had an increased weight of 94.6 kg (208.6 lb) but the range remained the same as before. These 1944 rockets were fired from mobile mountings but could also use the M-30. It is possible that the designation of the 310 mm rocket was TS-31.

**Data** (1944 version)

| | | | WEIGHT | 94.6 kg | 208.6 lb |
| --- | --- | --- | --- | --- | --- |
| LENGTH OVERALL | 1765 mm | 69.5 in | M.V. | 255 m/s | 837 ft/sec |
| DIAMETER | 310 mm | 12.2 in | RANGE | 4800 m | 5250 yards |

# M-31 Launcher

The first M-31 was fitted onto the GAZ-AA truck but after 1944 they were replaced by the GAZ-63. The M-31 consisted of two banks of six rectangular launching frames on a mounting similar to that used on the M-8 and M-13. Elevation and traverse controls were provided and an artillery dial sight was fitted. Jacks were provided at the rear for stabilising the chassis during firing. Like all the other Russian launchers a wide range of alternative vehicles were used to carry the M-31 and the above vehicles were only the 'standard' types. A variant of the basic M-31 was the M-31-UK which gave increased rocket dispersion.

**Data** (GAZ-63)

| | | |
| --- | --- | --- |
| LENGTH OF FRAMES | 2997 mm | 118 in |
| WIDTH OF FRAMES | 2133 mm | 94 in |
| LENGTH (inc. vehicle) | 6299 mm | 248 in |
| HEIGHT TRAVELLING | 3251 mm | 128 in |
| WIDTH | 2133 mm | 94 in |
| ELEVATION | 10° to 50° | |
| TRAVERSE | 20° | |

*M-31 launcher*

*M-31 310 mm launcher fitted to GAZ-AA truck*

# Other Russian Rockets

One rocket about which very little is known is the 280 mm (11 in) rocket produced in Leningrad during the Siege. Production began in 1942. References have also been found relating to a rocket weighing 57 kg (125.7 lb) being fired from a M-20 launcher which appears to have been similar to the M-13.

During 1942 a 120 mm (4.72 in) rocket was produced which weighed 14 kg (30.8 lb) and had a range of 5000 m (5470 yards). Nothing else can be discovered about this projectile.